BORIS

Günther Bosch

Willow Books
Collins
8 Grafton Street, London W1
1987

Willow Books
William Collins Sons & Co Ltd
London · Glasgow · Sydney
Auckland · Toronto · Johannesburg

First published in Great Britain 1987
© Verlag Ullstein GmbH 1986
© In the English translation
William Collins Sons & Co Ltd 1987

Photographs by Paul Zimmer, Thomas Exler,
Eckhard Herfort and Ullstein

British Library Cataloguing in
Publication Data
Bosch, Günther,
    Boris.
    1. Becker, Boris
    2. Tennis players—Germany—
    Biography
    I. Title
    796.342′092′4   GV994.B4/

    ISBN 0-00-218280-7

Filmset by Ace Filmsetting Ltd, Frome,
Somerset
Printed in Great Britain by
William Collins Sons & Co Ltd, Glasgow

CONTENTS

MY COACH BY BORIS BECKER

At first I couldn't stand my coach. He was National Trainer. What did *he* want, I wondered. Why was he butting in? I don't like teachers anyway. Why, how come? I don't believe anyone just because they're older or a teacher.

Günther Bosch didn't laugh with us kids. He kept himself aloof; he just watched. There were trainers who lived with us, went to discos with us or went out with girls ... nothing serious, just dancing.

But Günther Bosch just stayed in his room the whole time. He didn't come along. Once, at a training camp, we went to a restaurant with him. It was a wine-tasting session. You could drink as much wine as you wanted, it wouldn't cost you a penny ... Cola or Fanta cost money. Most of our training group were drunk after half an hour. I drank Cola, even though it cost money. Günther Bosch came over to me and said, 'You'll outlive them all.'

I didn't even think about it at the time.

People say all sorts of things. They all made fun of me because of my legs. 'Tennis is a running sport, you can't run.' Günther Bosch said, 'If you jump when you serve, your service will have more power. Jump eight inches higher.' When he was training me as National Trainer, we did a lot of sprinting. We did a lot of jumps. Three months later I wiped out the 25-year-olds – with my service.

Nowadays, if we have an argument, we make it up on court. We have our own language. I can't explain it. Guntzi is honest; he's never lied to me.

He runs with me, he's nearly fifty. I'm more powerful than him; but he's there beside me; 4000, 5000 metres, he's still there.

I can wipe him off the court, he hasn't got a chance; but he fights.

He jumps three feet in the air and says, 'Now you do it.' In Melbourne, there was this wall: I can't remember if it was at the tennis centre or on the way to the hotel. Every evening, he'd jump up and say, 'Jump higher.' We hopped like kangaroos.

You don't get anywhere on your own. On my own, I'm lazy. He winds me up, pushes me on. He's quite thin; but he has such willpower. Sometimes he unnerves me because he says nothing: 'What are you thinking, philosopher?' I ask.

Ion is direct, comes straight out with things. So do I. Guntzi thinks. Only at training sessions does he tell me what he was thinking. We were at a rock concert once: I'd taken my jumper off and my shirt, I was dancing with nothing on from the waist up. Next day on court, Guntzi said, 'Take your shirt off, dance!' I knew what he meant: he wanted me to be as relaxed as I'd been the night before. The thought came to him yesterday – and now he told me it.

I've read this book he's written. We did some of the chapters together. It's a book about coaching. He coaches me the way it says in the book. He's my coach.

'WHO IS THAT KID?'

The first time I saw Boris, he was playing tennis. He didn't look the kind of kid who played tennis: he had a round face, which his hair – a kind of pony-tail – made even rounder. He was overweight – baby fat, of course – with legs like a piano, by which I mean shapeless legs, with a lot of fat and no muscle.

Boris was nine years old.

He played a strange kind of tennis – he didn't use his feet. He threw himself towards the ball like a goal-keeper and raged when he didn't get it. A remarkable kid. I stopped and watched him. His knees were grazed, his arms sore.

'What's that kid's name?' I asked.

'Becker,' they said, 'Boris Becker.'

That was in Biberach. More than 50 youngsters were playing in front of the trainers of the German Tennis Association, to see who should be given further individual training, paid courses, invitations to international tournaments. The Association holds trials like this every year for young talented German tennis players.

Boris failed.

At that time, I was only deputy national trainer; I hadn't been in Germany for long, and I was only along as an observer. I could say what I

Boris using a forehand grip – at sixteen. Tongue slightly out between his lips, his stance one of concentration

thought, but it wouldn't count for much. I seem to remember talking about Boris's eyes. The trainers were going by a checklist: running, technique, many individual tests. There was nothing on the list about 'eyes' or 'concentration'.

When I think back today to that clumsy kid (in the 30-metre sprint, he was one of the last to waddle past the post), all I can see is his eyes. He didn't look like the other kids. He stared at each oncoming ball so hard that I thought: 'That's impossible in a kid'. How could a kid look so hard at the ball? Most kids' attention wanders all over the place, to whatever catches their attention: a car horn, a fly, laughter on the next court.

Off the tennis court, Boris was like any other kid, but as soon as he had the racket in his hand and the ball was coming over the net, he changed. His way of looking, the way his eyes work, this over-concentration is not something he learnt from me.

I have been living with Boris for three years. His parents entrusted me with their son when he was fifteen; later, at my suggestion, Ion Tiriac took over as his manager. Boris is on the way to being the number one in tennis. He has become a kind of world phenomenon. People cheer him everywhere – in America, Japan, Great Britain. At seventeen, he won at Wimbledon; and while I am finishing this book about him, I can hear his car starting below. We live next door to one another in Monte Carlo. I go out to the balcony and look down, and there is Boris, eighteen years old, threading his new black car

Seeing and hitting. A backhand swing. Boris has kept his sideways stance, unusual for his age. He is twelve. Most youngsters derive their strength and swing from turning the top half of their body. Boris is already playing the backhand stroke like an adult. **Right:** *Two years older and eight inches taller. His legs are more muscular. Notice again the way he looks at the ball. At the time, he wanted to be number one in his age group. He lost games that were as good as won, and learned that a game is never won or lost until the last ball*

No homesickness here. Boris is fourteen, flies to New York on his own, goes through customs alone, tells the taxi driver, 'Flushing Meadow'. He's playing in the Youth Tournament. **Above:** He blinks while changing ends. Boris was never homesick. The tennis court was his den. All courts are the same: home was wherever he was playing

Overleaf: Monte Carlo. Looking from the Palace down on to Millionaires' Bay – his home and mine

11

into the traffic. It's the middle of July: last week he won Wimbledon for the second time.

'Don't drive too fast!' I yell down.

He grins up at me, knows I'm on the balcony. No doubt that's why he revved up the motor. I don't like him driving so fast. He likes annoying me. Since the time when his parents entrusted him to me, he's grown over eight inches and is now more than six feet tall. His rounded features have turned into an angular face, his shoulders have widened, his hips narrowed.

While we were out jogging this morning, I asked him if it hurt when he failed at the trials at Biberach when he was nine. He shook his head.

It's remarkable how kids don't seem to be amazed by anything: everything is just the way it is. I'm forty-eight now, and I'm convinced that your childhood follows you like an invisible shadow your whole life through.

Many sports stars only became stars through hunger: Nastase, Muhamad Ali, Maradona, even Ion Tiriac ... Only the hungry become world champions. But Boris was hungry, too, although he was never short of food. Boris never had to drink bad water, or go hungry like Ion Tiriac or me – and yet he was still hungry. He was born in 1967: the times were good, his father was an architect.

Boris comes from a middle-class family, but his mother still knew what hardship was. Elvira Becker was a refugee child. That's important because she didn't spoil Sabine or Boris, her children, she didn't stuff them full of chocolate, cakes or sweets. So Boris still has good teeth. That might sound funny, but his teeth are part of his aura. He has teeth like an airline pilot,

Boris and I at eight in the morning, in Crans-Montana, Switzerland. High altitude training: 20 minutes' running, 40 minutes' exercise, shower, breakfast – and then on to court

15

with no fillings – strong, healthy teeth, which won't let any illness past them. He gets over everything quickly.

At Wimbledon, a year ago, he went to bed nearly every night sniffing, shivering, feverish, exhausted, with blood blisters: but the next morning he would be fine again. Every evening, Ion Tiriac was so desperate, he wanted to call the doctors to Boris's hotel room. 'He heals himself,' I calmed him down. 'He sleeps himself well.'

When Boris and I became a team, I fought my way through the thickets of his childhood. Tennis is a strange, mysterious sport. Why does a player's performance vary so wildly over a season, or even a tournament? I wanted to know what made Boris tick – even now, there are no secrets between us. He can't beat Lendl if he takes his problems on court with him. I drove to his house.

Leimen is in a beautiful setting. The tram rattles through the town, lovely old houses nestle by the roadside. From Heidelberg, the way to Leimen is by tram. A few metres from

By bike to the tennis court, by bike to school. Destination: 51 Nusslocher Strasse, his parents' home. **Right:** *Tennis mother Elvira Becker's second most important job: washing clothes, and washing yet more clothes*

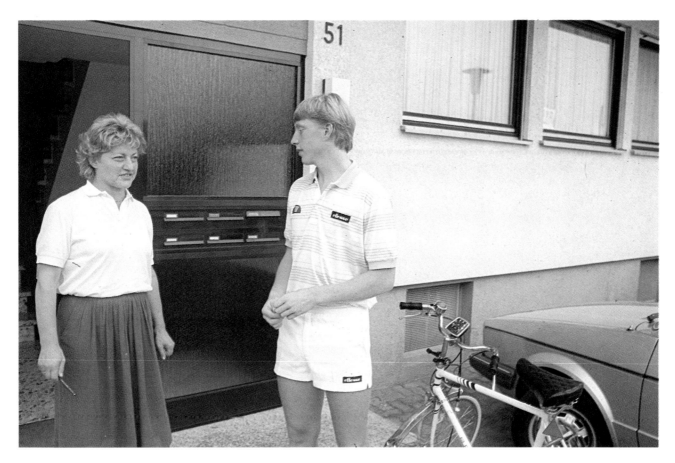

his parents' house is the Leimen Tennis Centre, built by his father, Karl-Heinz Becker.

Today, when I try to remember what it was like to be a child and hungry during the war, I can't do it. The same thing happens to Boris when I ask him what it was like to be hungry. After he failed at the trials, he played with the girls – he had degenerated into a kind of sparring partner for them. In principle, no-one worried, not even his parents. This, too, is part of his secret. Before I became his coach, Boris had never had a single individual training session. He was lucky to have parents without false ambitions: he was able to grow up as a tennis 'foundling', without being distorted.

He trained along with the others, just one of the crowd at the Leimen Tennis Centre. As a baby, he crawled around behind the courts where his parents were playing. The sound of tennis balls was part of his everyday life.

For some, the world is divided into good and bad people. But what is 'good'? You can divide the world into sportspeople and non-sportspeople. Sportspeople themselves would find that easy to understand: however young you are, whatever class you're in, if you're number ten, your ambition is to be number nine.

At nine or ten, Boris was free to do what he liked: throw himself around, dive for the ball, bloody his knees and arms: everyone laughed at this mad kid, no-one took him seriously. 'I was a clown,' Boris says about this period. 'I fetched Cola for the others, and when they laughed, I laughed too. It wasn't that bad, coach.'

But it was bad. He was very hungry – hungry in his mind. He still is.

The things that people like about his courageous, attacking style are rooted in his childhood. His childhood sharpened his already-keen gaze. Off the court, his eyes look normal, not unsettling: ordinary, pale-blue eyes. On court, they are like muscles, tensed, alert, precise, focussed on his opponent's face, fixed on it, getting to know it in every detail.

His gaze is like that of a sentry, always on the alert. Can eyes be face-shields? If I say that

Boris's best shots are defensive shots, the experts will think I'm mad for his service is his keenest attacking weapon, his returns daring attacking returns, his volleys deadly.

Boris attacks to defend himself. At the moment, he is in my opinion the only player in the world who can keep up the pressure without a break because he never stops defending himself.

Boris does not laugh while he is playing or make jokes on court like Connors, Noah or Leconte. Boris does not laugh on court. There were too many people laughing in the early days.

Often, during the tournaments the last year, I made notes for this book. Often I thought: 'No, it won't work. You can't describe Boris.' He'll be one thing today, then surprise you by being the opposite tomorrow. In the changing rooms after his second win at Wimbledon, he said, 'Guntzi,' – he was still out of breath, I think he was in the shower – 'Guntzi, you won't believe this, but losing is a worse feeling than winning ever is.' Only later did I realize what he meant: winning doesn't lift him as high as losing drags him down.

I was delirious with joy, even Ion was beside himself. After the winning ball, Ion hit me on the shoulder so hard that I nearly fell out of the box.

But, after winning Wimbledon for the second

Like a bird stooping on its prey. Eyes on the ball. The ball is the prey. Boris's arms are like pendulums, keeping his balance. The ball calls for two different feelings: here, getting ready for a forehand swing, Boris has to hate it, so as to be able to punish it. The next ball, on the other hand, may need to be handled more tenderly

time, Boris stood in the shower and talked about losing.

'Boris,' I asked, 'Aren't you pleased?'

'Yes,' he said, 'but I thought it would be bigger, better.'

Boris and I didn't hit it off for quite a while – it was a year or two before he came to trust me. While I was finding out about him – from his club trainer, his parents, his sister Sabine – he was also making enquiries about me. He questioned other players, questioned me – and the most fascinating thing was something I only learnt later: he asked my wife the same questions.

He wanted to know how I came to be a German although I was born in Romania. He asked how I met my wife. He asked how I felt when my daughter was born. He couldn't believe that I played a deciding match against Tiriac the evening before the birth, with my nine-months-pregnant wife looking on. 'What kind of people are you?' said Boris. 'I could never do that.' He was very disappointed in us. He even learnt Romanian secretly, so he could understand Ion and myself when we shouted odd fragments of Romanian at each other on court. That's how suspicious he was.

After training had ended of an evening, I had to be a story-teller. He never stops asking questions. 'Which did you speak first, German or Romanian? What were your teachers like? When did you start going out with girls? Was your father strict?' He's still asking questions today; he never stops.

Ion Tiriac and I come from the same town: the Romanians call it Brasov, but in German it's Kronstadt. It used to be in Austria-Hungary. It lies in a valley reached via a narrow mountain pass: a long, beautiful drive through the Carpathians. Kronstadt is a factory town of 200,000

The day Ion Tiriac saw Boris for the first time: the finals of the Youth Tournament in Monte Carlo. I'm congratulating Boris

inhabitants. The truck factory where Ion and I worked is still there, and of course the tennis courts where Ion and I met. I'm a Siebenburgen German; we still speak German at home.

When I was a child, there was still a German primary school and a German church. People called it the Black Church of Brasov because it was burnt down twice. Today the German minority is much smaller: many Germans have emigrated as I have, many have married Romanians and their children have forgotten all their German.

Ion is Romanian; he grew up in the same area as me. I grew up in very modest circumstances: my father was deported to Russia for many years, but at least he came back from the war. Ion lost his father when he was nine.

Sport was all there was for us; our stomachs drove us to sport. If you were good, you got privileges. If you were better, you got even more privileges. As a kid, I earnt my 'bani' (pocket-money) as a ball-boy. I got up at five in the morning and picked up the balls for the players. If they had a break, I was allowed a few shots. One of them said I had talent, and sometimes he would give me a game. I progressed quite fast: at seventeen, I was number seven in the men's list in Romania.

As I was training one afternoon, Ion came over to me on the court. He was fifteen, still at grammar school like me. 'Günther,' he said, 'give me your racket. I've just made a bet that I can beat him over there.' 'Him over there' was a very good player.

(Tiriac is always betting. Even today, he still has a bet before every match. 'A hundred dollars that Boris wins.' I always accept. It's become a fixation: he bets on Boris, I accept. I'm superstitious like that. I would never lay money on Boris. I'm happy to lose if he wins.)

So I said to Ion, 'Are you crazy? How are you going to beat him? You've never held a tennis racket in your life!' Ion was an ice-hockey player who also played table-tennis very well.

'I've bet a hundred bani,' he replied. One mark. That was a lot of money. I gave Ion the racket. He won. Like all ping-pong players, he played from the wrist, but he had a good sense of space and an amazing ball sense. A great talent. When he had won, I asked him if he wanted to learn to play tennis. He did. I taught him – not entirely for altruistic reasons: I needed a good sparring-partner myself. Within three years, he had overtaken me. And he was still in the Romanian national ice-hockey team, and took part in the Olympic Games in Innsbruck. But soon he was better at tennis than at ice-hockey. We were now playing together in the Davis Cup team – he as number one, I as number two (Nastase came later). Meanwhile, I had finished secondary school and started my athletics studies. I graduated with a thesis on 'The Psychology of the Serve' and became a trainer.

Boris has often asked me why I became his trainer. I told him that everyone has a goal, an ideal picture of how they would like to see themselves. I always wanted to play tennis like Boris. The tennis I played was like chess, thought out in the head. Precision playing on the line, from line to line, true tennis geometry, everything thought out in detail. I was faster than Boris, my tennis was faultless – but it was the kind of tennis that could be learnt by dint of hard work. That 'something extra', beyond the limit, was something I didn't have.

After the trials in Biberach, I lost sight of Boris. I became national trainer, working intensively with the men's team: Davis Cup, King's Cup. (My team won the Davis Cup twice.) I was particularly involved with one player, Uli Pinner. He became number nineteen in the world. But, in spite of all this success, Germany was not a tennis country. It is not my intention here to go over the endless discussions I had with the gentlemen from the DTB (German Tennis Association) – after all was said and done, we all wanted to win. But how? Through this youth work? Never. Through the National League Associations, who showered young players with money? Never. Had any German player ever struggled through the qualifying rounds of the major tournaments in the USA, Australia, England or France? None that I know of.

When my Davis Cup team lost 5-0 to the Czechs in 1982 – against Lendl and Smid – I was relieved as national men's trainer, and as 'national trainer without portfolio', I was able to realize one of my dreams. I looked for four 14/15-year-olds, and began training them. There's no point in saying that youth work is wrong, what they ought to do is such-and-such. The only way is to do things better yourself.

The four youngsters were Udo Riglewski, Patrick Kühnen, Karl Uwe Steeb (all now pretty good National League players) and Boris Becker. Not that Boris was number one in the group. I still didn't know much about him, I'd only seen him play a few times. Many people tried to put me off him. Even his association trainer said, 'You want *Boris*? He won't last two days.'

Boris was not exactly the sort of child parents or teachers would want, the sort who do everything their parents or teachers ask, try and fit in one hundred per cent, always understanding and just a little cunning: 'Yes, yes, you're right.'

Boris was not a calculating child. He threw his racket on the ground, yelled 'No!' a thousand times. He didn't put on an act. There are these kids who always toe the line, who will go through anything for their trainers, ready to make any sacrifice – just like in school. But when the teacher's not there, all hell is let loose.

So, now and then I would go outside the hall and try to look through the window and see what went on when I wasn't there. The 'good' kids were all failures. The training programme was forgotten, they were all just messing about.

Only Boris the lout kept on playing – he didn't care whether I was watching or not. That was something special; but it wasn't on the DTB checklist either.

There was something about this child that drew me. Even the way he cried. All children cry when they lose. But Boris's crying was terrible. He ranted, tore the shirt from his body, threw things around in the changing room. Most children cry because they're sorry for themselves. Boris cried because he hated himself. Once, when he was fourteen, he even smashed up his racket. I'd never seen anything like it: he smashed it against a post until it was in splinters.

That was at the Orange Bowl in Miami, at the

22

World Youth Championships. Boris was playing against an Italian; on paper, and in terms of results, he was the better of the two. At that time, there was already a 'Becker style': hit the ball just two inches inside the line. But that day all the balls that counted were landing just *behind* the line.

Smashing up a racket is a very unusual thing with youngsters of that age. They get maybe two or three rackets a year. A racket is a valuable thing. It was terrifying: Boris wasn't smashing his racket, but himself; because, for Boris, his racket is an extension of his arm.

This youngster has determined the course of my life.

His rackets lying in a heap on the ground. If they don't help him win, they get smashed. For Boris, rackets are living things: his friends, but sometimes friends he quarrels with. In his bag: anything up to five shirts, several sweatbands, saline tablets and energy bars

BORIS IS EIGHTEEN

'On night flight, Singapore Airlines, 22.11.85' ... I can't remember exactly where I wrote these notes. Were we over land or water? I wrote them sometime in the night, during our 25-hour flight to the Australian Open in Melbourne. 'Boris is sleeping. We celebrated his eighteenth birthday at 30,000 feet. I wished him good health: if he has that then there will be nothing to worry about.'

I had ordered a cake with eighteen candles. A year before, I would have had no idea how to go about this. A cake with candles in an aeroplane? Would they even let us light the candles? And then the stewardesses singing: 'Happy birthday, dear Boris!'

'I have a problem,' I told the ground hostess at Frankfurt. 'Boris will be eighteen during the flight, is there any way a cake ...?'

On the stroke of midnight, the stewardesses brought the cake. Winning at Wimbledon was like a magic wand.

Boris was bubbling over. When the minute hand showed that he was eighteen, he was more worked up than the first time he won at Wimbledon. 'Now I can take my driving test ... Where should I take it? In Germany? No, takes too long. We won't be in Germany that long. In New York? Yes, New York. Or maybe not, I'll take it in Monte Carlo. The week we're in Monte

Carlo ...' Now he has four licences: two American, one from Monte Carlo and an international one.

We ate lobster and caviare, Boris drank his first-ever glass of champagne.

'Guntzi, now I can make my own decisions, sign things myself.' Two years before, his parents had signed the contract with Ion Tiriac on his behalf. True, Boris had signed as well, but in legal terms his signature meant nothing.

The captain appeared for our birthday party, and the stewardesses – they all had to have a piece of cake. The captain invited Boris up on the flight deck, let him take the controls. Boris 'flew' the Jumbo.

'Wowee!' I heard him shout.

I have to admit I was afraid of this birthday – but perhaps fear is the wrong word: I was concerned about the new life that was just beginning.

Boris had always wanted to be a professional. His mother would have liked him to take his A-levels and play tennis more as a hobby. But at fourteen or fifteen, Boris wasn't listening. Ion and I had made it quite clear to him what it would mean, the sacrifices he would have to make to be a professional. 'OK, OK, OK,' he said. He was obsessed with becoming a professional. Five hours' training a day, a life that revolved around tennis, on the scales every day, never letting up, never letting your body go ... It begins with the food and ends with sleep. There are a lot of things you have to do without.

At fifteen, you don't mind doing without,

Arriving in Melbourne. The first present: a cake for his eighteenth birthday. He was happy until the first round: then he got knocked out

you've no idea what it means. As a boy, Boris had read everything about Borg, Connors and Vilas. He wanted to be like them, to live a harder, more Spartan life.

Giving up normal life is a major problem. Is this something you can do to a child? I can't imagine a world-class tennis player combining the high life and the life of a tennis player and keeping his performance up for long. In the top ten, it's the mental attitude that wins the deciding points; the Latin word *mens* means 'spirit, soul, common sense'. Taken as a whole, it means the power of concentration. (This, by the way, is why Wilander isn't playing like he used to. His thoughts are elsewhere. He has a girlfriend in New York, a beautiful model, he has found how sweet life can be outside tennis. This is a very big problem. On the one hand, it's perfectly normal and human for a young man to have a girlfriend, to have a public life. It's only human for him to want her, think of her. But, on the other hand, it causes damage. A lot of damage.)

Mariana, Bjorn Borg's separated wife, was my pupil in Romania. Before she married Borg, she went with him from one tournament to the next. I asked Mariana what their life was like together. 'I washed Bjorn's clothes, I woke him up. I knocked him into shape before each match. I packed his bags. When he didn't feel like speaking, I kept quiet. I was like a second coach.' Perhaps it can work like that. But there aren't many girls like Mariana.

In any case, a girl upsets the rhythms of an athlete's life. She is in his thoughts, he must spend time on her. Things get bad when you give up a tournament because of a girl. Bad for the player, but also bad for the girl. Both start feeling guilty.

Boris was a child when he let himself in for the professional life – and I had helped him do it. Now he was eighteen; and I felt a bit guilty as though it was all my fault.

I had no plan, no tried and tested plan: 'if a seventeen-year-old wins at Wimbledon, use plan B ...'.

I myself was groping around in the dark. I had as little idea as Boris of what it meant to win at Wimbledon.

In a single afternoon, Boris had become a hero to anyone with a television set. Was it two or three hundred million people watching the first time he won at Wimbledon?

Who knew what would happen next? 30,000 people welcomed Boris to his home town, the media went wild, television, papers ... An hour's interview with Boris cost 150,000 marks, the President took part in a sports programme on TV on his account. Neither of us knew anything of the red carpets, the obligations, the contracts with Philips, Deutsche Bank, Puma, Coca-Cola which followed. As far as all this was concerned, we were idiots.

I was just the ordinary trainer of an ordinary kid, who admittedly hit balls like I'd never seen before.

There's one ball which is unbelievable – his return of service. Lendl, after Boris the hardest server, is serving. Before the ball can rise after hitting the ground, Boris has found it.

It's like two cars crashing at top speed. Boris hits a return too fast for the naked eye to see. There are photos in this book showing Boris's face during a return. It looks like a rock.

After his win, his first at Wimbledon, there were times when his face scared me. Unless Boris was on television, in front of the cameras, his face became impersonal, like a mask. It was the face he wore when travelling, when flying to the airport in the helicopter, when passing straight through customs. The face he wore in

'Go on, wave,' I said to Boris on the balcony at Leimen Town Hall. 30,000 people were there to welcome him home after his first win at Wimbledon

28

Left: *As we drove into Leimen, Boris had cramp. He could hardly move. He didn't react: he didn't look left or right. The crowd were throwing flowers; fathers held their children up for him to touch. It took Boris a long while before he surfaced, until he understood the joy that people felt*

Above: *Inscribing the Golden Book, with Mayor Ehrbar behind in ceremonial dress. 'I felt like a little tennis ball,' Boris said later*

restaurants – looking at the wall. The face he wore getting out of cars. It wasn't his fault the way he changed. After his first win at Wimbledon, Boris just couldn't imagine himself belonging to us normal people any more. The people staring at him, reaching out for him, and the girls of course, all those girls, hysterical, crazy, waiting for hours outside hotels.

Is it fair to do this to a child? I mean, aren't you cheating him out of his real life, real friendship, his first sweetheart? How can he find out what's real and what's sham? The girls are simply offering themselves; all he has to do is take. Others must fight for girls, 'earn' love and friendship. He gets them served up on a plate, free. He doesn't have to do anything. That can't be good for a child's development. That's why I said I felt a bit guilty.

There was so much I wanted to wish for him on his birthday ...

During the flight, I suddenly thought of how he had danced once, and that made me feel calmer.

Boris was fourteen at the time, it was around Easter, during a training camp on Majorca. We were not alone. There were boys and girls from Berlin there, many others from the different DTB associations. Everyone had a record-player, the boys and girls were dancing. Boris too. On his own for a few minutes at first, with no-one noticing. Then they formed a chain.

Do you know 'Zorba's Dance'? It was like that. An incredible harmony. Boris was moving as a single unit, body and soul were one at that moment. It was an incredible experience for me. What was all that rubbish about leg-work, I thought. No-one with lazy legs moves like that. All those years, we had been training his body, but forgotten his soul. There were many who danced better than he did, with more flamboyant, attractive movements. But there was no-one dancing that evening with more harmony or more abandonment. That vision of Boris dancing cheered me up on his birthday. We have to find what is harmonious in everything, I thought. Finally I went to sleep. In the next seat, Boris had already been asleep for ages.

THE HARMONIOUS SERVICE

The serve, coming at the other player at over 150 miles an hour, is Boris's best shot. I'd like to begin this chapter with an interview which Boris gave after his second win at Wimbledon.

Reporter: Boris, why do you need a coach?
Boris: To get in the right mood, the right feeling.
Reporter: How do you mean?
Boris: Some days, I can't get the right feeling. I can't serve. I don't know why. Then the trainer has to stand there and make sure I get the feeling back, even if I have to serve a hundred times.
Reporter: What kind of a feeling is that?
Boris: A nice, harmonious feeling.

I was present when Boris gave those replies. I was pleased he used the word 'harmonious'. Boris's serve is not just a 'wham-bam', as aggressive reporters call it. When it works, it is the result of the greatest harmony. In the seven singles matches at Wimbledon the second time, Boris hit 102 aces – more than any other player before him. A quarter of these he hit with his second ball, as if he had a third to fall back on if things went wrong. I'll try and explain Boris's best shot.

Concentration before serving. The ball has been thrown up: all the tension is in the left hand. The right hand, relaxed, holds the racket. The chain reaction begins

It begins with things which at first sight have nothing to do with tennis. On the Sunday of the Finals, we were both humming 'Today is the sweetest day of my life ...' over breakfast at the Londonderry Hotel. This song, this grotesque claim, was how we felt: 'Today is the most beautiful day of my life'. I don't know which of us started humming first – Boris or me. But anyway, it became our Finals' song.

How can I say how it felt that day? Imagine a very important day in your life, exams, A-levels perhaps – and then multiply that feeling by 100. I only know a few people (players) who can cope with such a feeling. During Wimbledon, we could read the question in everyone's eyes: is he a hero or just a flash in the pan?

It began right from the morning. The waiter said, 'Good luck, Boris.' We saw his eyes. The thousands of people we met. 'Good luck, Boris.' We saw their eyes.

The millions of people in front of their TVs, the 15,000 on the Centre Court, the reporters, the click-click-click of the cameras ... Some people wanted to see the hero fall. We could feel that. The celebrities in the Royal Box. The German President, the Prime Minister, the Duke and Duchess of Kent – and Boris was playing Lendl, the number one in the world in tennis.

In the changing rooms, we went on singing: 'Today is the most beautiful day in my life' – and played ice-hockey. The changing-room door was the goal, a tennis ball was the puck and our rackets the sticks.

Boris hit sixteen aces in the Final. Once, he

was serving at 0-40 down. He won game and set with three aces in a row.

How does he do it while under so much pressure? His serve is a round, self-contained action, which is divided into six phases.

Phase 1: Concentrating on looking at the other player: already trying to fool him, trying to make him think the ball's going one way, trying to lure him the wrong way. It's like playing poker with your eyes. Boris holds the racket with both hands, level in front of him. He stares at the other player, fixing him with his gaze.

Phase 2: Just below hip height, the left hand now lets go of the racket. The right arm prepares for the swing. His gaze moves from his opponent. He draws back the racket in secret, behind his body, so that his opponent won't see which way he is going to hit the ball.

Phase 3: With his fingertips, Boris throws the ball high in the air. We've changed levels. He now throws it higher, without the earlier anti-clockwise twist. He is completely at peace, very quiet – the quiet before a storm.

Phase 4: His body is like a wheel hurtling down a hillside, unstoppable. Boris arches his back, bends his knees, prepares for the swing forwards. The movement is open and smooth, the interplay of muscle tension and relaxation.

Phase 5: At the right moment, which he alone can feel and decide, he leaps six inches in the air with his legs crossed and, with the force of the leap behind him, hits the ball.

Phase 6: In hitting the ball, he hurtles forwards and reaches the net as soon as he touches the ground. That's it – but is it real?

I have no idea how many serves Boris and I have practised together. 30,000 a year, 40,000? It must be around 100 a day plus the innumer-

able 'dry serves' Boris practises everywhere – on our terrace in Monte Carlo, out walking, even in the plane. Again and again, he practises his coordination of the two main movement sequences, throwing the ball and drawing back his arm. He just hints at them, they are invisible movements. They weren't my idea; he thought them up himself. As I am writing this, Boris is number three in the world, and it is fascinating watching his determination to serve better tomorrow than he does today.

I don't like people watching us during training, because for us training is a very intimate thing. We yell at each other and argue. You'd think we were madmen. When reporters are around, we hide our feelings, 'act normal'. No reporters are around now.

Five serves Boris makes – and five times the ball lands in the net.

'Smile Lendl. Good Luck Boris.' The Wimbledon Finals 1986. Two girls, two wishes on the same T-shirts. Two hours and two minutes later, Boris was smiling. He'd won Wimbledon for the second time

Overleaf: *Fireworks: the camera captures Boris's explosive service*

I yell, 'Throw the ball higher, for heaven's sake!'

He yells back, 'No, it feels good!'

That happens sometimes. He feels good, but the ball still lands in the net or behind the line.

I tell him, 'Are you crazy? That's five serves you've screwed up.'

Boris: 'But it feels right.'

I yell, 'I can't see what you feel. Tell me how it feels!'

He yells back, 'The speed is right, the rhythm is good, my shoulders are loose, I can feel the timing.'

Wham – straight in the net again.

So it goes on, hour after hour. He changes his shirt – the old one is wringing with sweat – and is tensed up and aggressive. But we carry on, on and on. I correct him: 'Now you're throwing too far to the left ... now two inches too short ... now you were late in jumping.'

It's enough to drive you mad. I yell what I see and he yells what he feels. That's the way it goes, day after day. Boris has never yet broken off a training session.

Anatomy of a service: it looks so simple, but it is as complicated as a watch mechanism. A combination of stillness, rhythm, jumping, power, violence and precision. Boris's service shows his self-confidence, and acts as an indicator of his game

BORIS AND HIS OPPONENTS

The Top Ten is like a myth, a closed society. If you're not one of them, they don't know you. When Boris was number 20, Connors wouldn't speak to him. In the changing room, Boris had to put his things right at the back, and wait patiently until it was his turn with the masseur. In Wimbledon there is a communal changing room for the lower orders; the big boys keep to themselves. It was only when Boris got into the semi-finals a year ago that he was allowed into the seeds' changing rooms.

When one of the Top Ten speaks, others keep quiet: that is an unwritten law. When Wilander talks about a tournament, no-one else dares butt in. A number 60 never goes on court before a number five. The Top Ten lead a secret life – and number one the most secret life of all. Number one goes into isolation, guarding and fostering the mystery around himself, trying to be an insoluble riddle.

What does anyone know about Lendl or McEnroe? Borg is another mystery man. The press may talk about the houses they live in, who lives with them, how much they earn a year. But no-one ever learns the things that really count: what they think, how they work, their agonies, where they get their motivation.

Ivan Lendl, the number one – and Boris. Here, at an exhibition match in Berlin, they were still smiling at one another. Now that Boris is number two in the world, things have grown cold between them

Even their trainers give nothing away. The Top Ten's trainers are just as closed-off towards other players' trainers. There is only one place where the Top Ten have to lift the veil: on court.

Boris was not yet fifteen, a leather purse around his neck with his pocket-money and passport in it, when we took a good look at the Top Ten from the stands. Alongside the Grand Slam tournaments – Roland Garros in Paris, Wimbledon, Flushing Meadow and Melbourne – there are the Youth Tournaments. When Boris had finished his match, we went over to look at the big boys.

I remember that Connors hit himself on the thigh with his racket during the match. I remember Boris's eyes. He was fascinated. Medical evidence exists that you can get 'high' without drugs. While still a child, Boris saw Connors inflicting pain on himself so as to whip more adrenalin into his blood. The matches with Connors taught Boris a great deal. He saw it wasn't enough just to play good tennis. You have to be able to put yourself in a special state to achieve the outstanding.

This year (1986), Boris beat Connors at his own game in Chicago. Boris had blood-blisters under the skin on his feet: but he trampled around on them before the match to hurt himself even more. Afterwards, the experts said they had never seen such an aggressive match. Connors fought as never before – and Boris fought like Connors.

After the match, we could hear Connors raging in his changing rooms. Even on the

Opposites: Ivan Lendl, an athlete with power; and McEnroe, the genius with feeling. For me, Boris is a combination of both

massage table, he was full of hate – not for Boris, but for himself. That's how different the Top Ten are – and how alike.

John McEnroe always has trouble with photographers, spectators and umpires – launching real tirades of hate. And then – we've seen this very clearly – playing better than before the argument. That too is a way of getting the adrenalin going. It was noticeable that in his weak periods John would always look for an argument, break it off at the climax, calm down again in the space of a few seconds and then be at his most dangerous.

Boris has been longing to play him for over a year. He has often said, 'I hope he comes back, I want to play him.' For him, John McEnroe is a great challenge. Let me explain. He is a creative player, a genius.

After a seven month break when he plunged to level seven in the ATP (Association of Tennis Professionals') computer world list, John McEnroe is now back with the pack in the Top Ten.

He came back fully trained, well prepared. In his first game at the Stratton Mountain tournament in Vermont, we could see this was no half-hearted comeback attempt.

On Saturday, 9 August 1986, the day arrived. John and Boris met in the semi-finals. The whole US tennis press was there, it was going out live on all American TV stations. Two hours and 32 minutes later, Boris had beaten John McEnroe 4-6, 7-5, 7-6. It was very close, very dramatic.

The fighters: Jimmy Connors, Boris's idol, because he always fights and never gives up. What is so impressive about Kevin Curren is his powerful serving and stamina.

'Listen, John,' the American reporters said at the press conference afterwards, 'What have you got against Boris? You said some very unfriendly things to him during the match.'

McEnroe looked up. 'Yes, I demand that he shows me more respect.'

What had happened?

The pack which he had left as the deposed number one, had re-formed. There was a new lead wolf: Lendl. And there was a new member: Boris, who bit everyone. They are all wolves, even Boris.

During the match, McEnroe swore at Boris, did everything he could to break his concentration. And then, in the tie-break in the last set, Boris bit back. McEnroe had three match points against Boris. The crowd were going wild. For most of them, McEnroe had already won. Then Boris lifted his finger and signalled: hold on. Nothing has been settled yet.

The crowd fell quiet. McEnroe couldn't believe his eyes. Who did this kid think he was? For McEnroe, Boris was 'the kid'. 'Kid, kid, kid!' he yelled at him during the game. McEnroe had three match points, the game in his pocket – and then this eighteen-year-old kid lifts his finger and says 'Hold on'.

And then Boris actually pulled back the three match points, danced his 'Boris shuffle', clenched his fists. 6-all. Then McEnroe had match point again. 8-7. But then Boris pulled back and overhauled the incredulous McEnroe to win 10-8.

Unbelievable. The stadium shook. A standing ovation.

McEnroe was still raging after the game. 'How dare he clench his fists? When I was eighteen, I had respect for Connors or Laver. Boris is a lout.'

There were two more biting sessions outside the Centre Court. Boris was asked by reporters:

'Boris, are you going to marry a movie star?' (McEnroe is married to Tatum O'Neal.)

Boris: I think I'm going to marry a woman.
The reporters: What do you think of McEnroe as a person?
Boris: I've always said he's a good player. I've never said he's a good person.

I'm certain Boris would never have answered that way a year before. A lot of things have happened in the wolf-pack since he broke in.

Does Boris dislike McEnroe? Far from it. He

Opponents and friends: Mats Wilander, the marathon player, with perhaps the best backhand in the world, number two before Boris came along. Stefan Edberg, who plays like Boris: temperamental, but who plays 100 per cent attacking tennis

likes him. He will only bite him on court or near it. However big he once was as a player, he would never give McEnroe a point out of respect or pity.

Anyway, the McEnroes came to see us the next day. First McEnroe senior, then Tatum O'Neal, then finally John. John apologized. They shook hands.

There is also an interesting parallel here. When Borg retired, he tried to make a comeback in Stuttgart a year later. He was smashed by Henri Leconte. He didn't even let him save face.

I asked Boris if he would have spared Borg, for whom he had great respect. When he was seven or eight, Boris would get up in the middle of the night to watch Borg playing on television; he bought tapes on which Borg told children about himself.

'No,' said Boris, 'I would have slaughtered him the same way.'

I think players like Boris – for one thing, because he livens things up, he's someone to go after, to shoot down. Winning against Boris has something special about it. Apart from that, Boris is fair, plays fair: for instance, he has never aimed a shot at his opponent's body, like Lendl or McEnroe. 'Liking' is one thing. Friendship is something that scarcely has a chance. After all, they're all out to get each other.

In the Top Ten, only the Swedes are an exception. Boris feels most at home with them. Stefan Edberg, number six in the world, is possibly a

Still more Swedes: Anders Jarryd, the weasel: the lightning-reaction net player. Always a close-run game for Boris. Joakim Nystrom, the butterfly, runs as if he's flying – and never pulls a face

kind of friend. The Swedes travel as a group from tournament to tournament. Jarryd, Wilander, Nystrom and Edberg train together, mess around together, crack jokes, laugh, have fun – but on court they fight each other without quarter for money and points. Boris and I often watch them. They even warm each other up before matches. I don't mean knocking the ball about before a match begins. They can play against each other in the evening and train together the next morning.

How can that be possible, we ask ourselves?

Both Boris and I need an 'enemy'. Anyone he

The flamboyant and the nobody: Yannick Noah stands for power and showmanship; he can't be out-lobbed, and owns an incredibly powerful pair of legs. Schapers, the Dutchman, stands for Boris's unnecessary defeats

plays against is our enemy. No quarter given, or taken. A year ago, all I needed to do was to mention a player's name two or three days before a match, and Boris would become aggressive. Sometimes, while training, he would yell out the name of his next opponent. 'Annacone, I'm ready.' Things could build up until the first outbreak of sweat on court.

We have often discussed the Swedes. They're just different, that's all. Perhaps their peaceful countryside has left its mark on them, the wide open spaces, the clear sky – that's the only thing I can think of. All Swedes, including Edberg, are marathon players: they play their way calmly and stoically over five sets – I call it the 'reindeer gait'. Remarkable …

For instance, Edberg is now going out with Wilander's old girlfriend – but they're still the best of friends. How do they manage it? Edberg and Wilander face each other in the final of the

Grand Slam tournament in Melbourne. Edberg wins. The same evening, we see them happily drinking together. It makes you envious.

Stefan and Boris knew each other as kids. They played in tournaments together. Until Boris was sixteen, he had never beaten Stefan. At an ATP tournament in Rosenheim, Stefan slept in the changing rooms in a sleeping bag. Either he was broke or there were no more rooms. When Boris saw him, he asked, 'Can we help you? Do you need anything?'

They are definitely friends. If they meet at tournaments, they train together, and play one another in the evenings. I'm pleased they're friends – but then again, I'm not. Stefan plays like Boris: an aggressive serve and volley player, his keenest future opponent. I have a feeling that in the struggle for the world tennis throne, the main battles are going to be between these two. An inner voice tells me Stefan shouldn't be allowed to get to know Boris so well when he has grown up.

Boris still has faith in the world around him: that's good, but sometimes dangerous. He plays the way he is: not maliciously or underhandedly. I hope he manages to stay the way he is.

Sometimes I have the feeling that when he loses his 'innocence' and realizes that the world we live in is not all good, it will change his game. I hope he keeps on playing as innocently and pluckily for a long time, for that's the way he is. Of course, one or two people have sometimes pulled the wool over his eyes.

Two years ago, for instance, the day before their singles match in Rome, Noah told him, 'Boris, I'm pulling out of the doubles tomorrow. I've hurt myself. Let's just have a good game tomorrow.' Boris wished him better. The next day, Noah did in fact turn up for the singles with a big plaster – but what happened? Noah got well and truly stuck in, ran around like a madman and swept Boris off the court. Boris didn't have a clue what had happened. Hadn't Noah told him he had hurt himself? There was no way Noah was injured – he'd just taken Boris for a ride. One-up. But to whom?

World class tennis is all in the mind. Seventy to eighty per cent of it is a test of nerves. After all, Borg didn't stop playing because he was out of condition: he stopped playing because his nervous energy was all used up.

And now it seems the same thing is happening with McEnroe. When he got knocked out by Annacone in his comeback attempt in the first round of the US Open, he said, 'It's dark inside my head. Unfortunately, there's no light switch I can use. For eight or nine years, the light was bright for me, then it flickered a bit; maybe I'm at the point where Bjorn Borg finished with tennis.' I sometimes think there are special tennis cells inside the brain: if you don't discharge them, they can't recharge.

But how can you relax? You can take long breaks between tournaments; that's one way. You can fill the breaks with things which are nothing to do with tennis: read, go to the theatre, be with people who are interested in other things. We've tried that; but Boris is not a bookworm or a keen theatre-goer. I'm all for his passion for music. After a rock concert, it's as though he's been reborn. The main thing is to be able to forget yourself, even if only for a few hours.

Another equally important thing is not to go against Nature. Cells help themselves by cracking up occasionally. Those are the positive outbreaks on court, the rages, smashing up rackets. Borg never lost his cool – maybe that's why his cells died off so quickly. He stopped at twenty-six. Boris – we hope! – will still be playing at thirty.

All players crack up at some time, and they all do it in their own way. When Lendl loses his cool, he gets faster. All his actions are carried out in overdrive. He tries shots he would normally never dare try, such as a drop shot from the baseline for instance. The sort of stroke no-one should ever try against someone of Boris's stamina. When you lose your cool, you can't think. When it happens to McEnroe, he suddenly starts playing from the baseline, stops going up to the net. Psychologists would be interested to note that players suddenly do the opposite of where their strength lies. They start playing against themselves.

This 'playing against yourself' was one of the problems we faced until Wimbledon II. Until Wimbledon II, Boris Becker's worst opponent was not Lendl, but Boris Becker.

HOW BORIS BECAME BORIS

Boris wasn't his normal self when he won Wimbledon. He has this to say about what happened at Wimbledon in 1985: 'It was like a trance, a dream.'

I can still see us sitting by his bed. The game against Nystrom had been interrupted, it was his third singles match after winning against Pfister and Anger. He had a slight temperature. He lost the first set to Nystrom, but won the second after a tie-break. Then it got dark. The match was postponed, to be carried on on Monday, 44 hours later.

'Don't worry, you've got nothing to lose,' Ion Tiriac and I said. 'Nystrom is number eight in the world, there's no shame in losing against a seed when you're unseeded.'

It was at that point that the dream began; but we had no idea it was beginning.

Were there any signs of what was happening? None. Today, I can say, 'Yes, perhaps.' But I don't know. In January that year, Boris had won the Young Masters tournament in Birmingham and then the warm-up tournament for Wimbledon at Queens. But this was Wimbledon, where only the best played.

Monday came around fast. Boris won the third set 6-1. He was playing without any sign of nerves. In the fourth set, Nystrom woke up and

---

Boris loves the sun, but when he's playing, it's his enemy. He has to play with his eyes open: he mustn't squint

won in straight games. The fifth set. Nystrom was leading 5-4. The normal thing would have been for Boris to have lost both game, set and match: a perfectly normal thing for an unusually fighting, unusually gifted seventeen-year-old.

But by that time we were well into the dream. Boris pulled level. 5-all. I always say this is where the mystical game began.

Boris's tennis lost its balance, its constancy. It became incredibly vulnerable, but at the same time pitilessly hard for a seventeen-year-old. He served double faults, lay on the ground, lost his service. His face was the face of a child: I couldn't bear it any more. Nystrom was leading 6-5, using his experience, his superior running ability. Boris was 'dying', as we say in tennis.

And then the 'miracle' happened. Boris broke Nystrom. He didn't make a song and dance about taking the game from him. He broke him physically. It was unbelievable. 6-all. Nothing was normal any more.

Boris hurled one ace at Nystrom after another. The set ended 9-7.

In the evening, Boris was ill in bed once more: shivering, feverish. He complained he couldn't move. 'Go to sleep,' I calmed him. I know how quickly he can sleep himself well. He had just one night in which to get better. Tim Mayotte, his next opponent, would be waiting for him the next day.

Tim Mayotte is a typical American fighter: six feet tall, a fully-trained athlete. They fought a very hard, aggressive match: 6-3, 4-6, 6-7 …

Once again, the spectre of defeat was looming over Boris; once again, the next set was – to use Boris's own words – 'Death and destruction'.

By this time, I think, there were a million Germans watching on TV for the first time. For many, it was the first time they'd ever watched tennis; most of them had no idea what the rules were, how the scoring went, and were hearing the name Boris Becker for the first time. What they saw was a seventeen-year-old, a kid, fighting for all or nothing.

Later, Ulrich Kaiser, the sports columnist, whose opinion I value, would write: 'You don't become a star by winning just like that, there has to be a bit of pain involved, you have to be pretty much "down" at first and fight like mad to make it end well. This is the way the whole film industry works: they call it the "happy ending".'

OK, so life is a film.

At 6-5, after two hours and 50 minutes, Boris twists his left foot, falls over and doesn't get up.

'It's nothing serious!' I yell down at him.

A year before, Boris had dropped out of Wimbledon in the third round with a double torn ligament in his left ankle. During a match, different memories are continually flashing through a player's head. He may remember a successful forehand in a hopeless situation. In a tight spot, this image flashes before him, and he plays the same shot again.

When Boris fell over, the torn ligaments flashed through his mind. He turned his face away. I had the feeling that he had a picture of himself the year before, being taken off in a wheelchair.

'It's nothing!' I roared down from the stands. 'Take your time out.' (A player can have three minutes time out if he has hurt himself.)

I was sitting in my track-suit. Ion Tiriac was in mufti: tie, made-to-measure suit. Boris insisted I dress like him. He said, 'We're the workers. You're the worker up there, I'm the worker down here.' Ion was 'the President'.

'Come on!' I roared, 'Keep on playing!'

I know how far he can push himself because I've played with him outside. I don't need a doctor to tell me if he's hurt himself. I'm right there alongside him. I felt the step he took when he fell over. Nothing was broken, or torn, or even strained. It was a perfectly normal fall.

Boris was sitting on his seat. He had taken his sock and shoe off. Where was the tournament doctor?

'Time,' said the umpire. The three minutes were up.

'Where's the doctor?' roared Boris.

'Play on!' I screamed.

Ion Tiriac was looking at me as though he couldn't believe his eyes. So was Boris. He was really in pain.

'Go on!' I roared. He believed me, not his pain. He lost the game.

Finally, the ATP masseur, Bill Norris, arrived. He'd got caught up in the crowd. He put a plaster on Boris.

Boris got up, took a few steps, put his weight on his left foot. It was OK. Change ends.

Boris signalled to Tim Mayotte: 'Play on.'

The score was 6-all. Tie-break.

Why am I talking about the past here? Because, after the first time at Wimbledon, every game Boris played was judged by that standard. Every game he played had to be as extraordinary. No more losing, no more weakness. Once a hero, always a hero.

What was this dead-end we'd let ourselves be pushed into? In Australia, he was knocked out in the first round by Schapers, number 180 in the world. How can you lose to number 180? Everyone had Wimbledon I in their minds, the 'mystical' Boris, lying on the ground and performing miracles.

Tim Mayotte to serve. He now looked certain to win. Boris was hurt – this had to be the end. Mayotte blew his service. 6-all. Tie-break.

Running back to the centre. Boris is hunted from one corner to the other. Wimbledon '85

Left: *Boris clenches his fist. He shouts at himself, 'Yes, go on!' He wants to hear his strength. His face is aggressive: you can't fight joyfully*

Above: *Boris unhappy. He throws down his racket, argues with the umpire. I tell him to let his temper out. 'Don't swallow it: that'll hamper your game.'*

In a tie-break, the points are counted one at a time. The first player to reach seven wins game and set, provided he has a two-point lead.

After the first point, each player serves twice in a row – a 'shoot-out'.

I can still see myself sitting there with ice-cold hands. If Mayotte won the tie-break, that was the end of the film. You wouldn't have believed my face, sitting there with Ion in the stands. Now and then, Boris would signal to me: 'Calm down, coach'. He could feel how cold my hands were.

In a tie-break, there are no benevolent spirits you can pray to, it's not a poker game or voodoo.

A player must be peaceful and calm inside. He must open the door and go quietly into the room. Yes, I think that's it.

Boris won the tie-break.

Now it was anyone's game again, they had each won two sets. The next set would be the deciding one.

Boris slaughtered Mayotte 6-2.

He played the ball as if in a dream. One paper wrote, 'Mayotte went off the court destroyed.'

Boris limped off the court. He was in the quarter-finals, in the last eight. Within an hour, the euphoria of winning collapsed. Then there were only moans, whimpers.

'Why me? Dear God, it wasn't my fault. Why can't I walk any more? Christ, my leg ...'

He lay on the massage table, being given electrotherapy. The tournament doctor, an orthopaedic specialist, put a new support bandage on. 'Guntzi, I haven't broken anything, have I ...?'

On the way back to the hotel, he was leaning on me. Once more, he was shivering slightly, fever blisters on his lips. I massaged him, stayed with him. Now and then I would talk about Leconte, his next opponent.

'Oh God, I can't, I can't walk ...' Henri Leconte had knocked Lendl out of the tournament.

Ion Tiriac organized the medical equipment, so we could give Boris electrotherapy that evening. Doctors were standing by. Ion pressed buttons, showing his inimitable organizational talent: Boris got the full treatment.

'Leconte gets high on playing,' I said. 'Don't let

him get a foot in. Don't take any notice of him. You'll win if you dictate the game.'

Could Boris hear what I was saying?

Normally, I have a habit of holding a long discussion the day before a game on the other player's strength. I build the other player up into an elephant; on the day of the match, he then seems like a mouse. On the day of the match, I only talk about Boris's strength. I want him to win before he even goes on court.

But could he hear what I said at all?

Wimbledon I broke all the rules. Nothing was normal any more.

I waited until Boris was asleep, then went to my room. Boris's pulse was slow. At rest, his heart beats 37 times a minute: this helps him go into a deep sleep.

Many top athletes' pulses are slow like that. For instance, if we're in a plane, Boris will start yawning straight away. Five minutes later, he'll be asleep. Nothing affects his sleep; he sleeps just as well before a match as in a plane. It may even be that he sleeps better before a match. He really dreams his way to winning. He imagines match points, the balls he will win with. Dozing, he pictures himself winning against Leconte. He's been doing that since he was a child, it's his lullaby. I only found that out gradually. Psychologists would love Boris: doing everything right seems to come naturally to him, it just happens without him realizing it. No-one told him how to do it.

In the morning, we trained, he ran a bit, we just had a few shots. His movements were flowing. In the afternoon came the match. Boris played as if it were a fresh summer's day. 7-6, 3-6, 6-3, 6-4.

How did I feel? I can't say. Now and then I would think, 'There's something wrong here. We're in the semi-finals.'

Ion was sandbagging us. Boris and I were living in a vacuum. Here's his room, I'm clearing it up. Shirts, training gear, socks, rackets, massage creams, cassettes, Walkman, jeans – all in a heap. Our chess game is on the table. The hotel switchboard has been told not to put any calls through. Ion is watching over us.

I like it when we play chess before a match.

Chess forces you to think two or three moves ahead. I try and convince Boris that life doesn't just exist in the present. Life means looking ahead. By now, Boris is better at chess than I am. Of the three of us, first I was the best at chess, followed by Ion and then Boris. Now Boris is the best, then me, then Ion.

We didn't play chess for long. After ten minutes, Boris took the figures off the board.

Anders Jarryd was disturbing our thinking: he was our next opponent.

Anders Jarryd was number six in the world. I hate the world rankings: they're intimidating. At that time, Boris was number 20. On paper, we had no chance.

We automatically talked about the service, Boris's greatest weapon.

What was good or bad at that moment? No-one could say. Boris had long since taken me with him on his magic trip. We were completely insane. Boris whimpered, said he couldn't take another step as long as he lived, then, the next moment, 'I'll kill that Jarryd!'

Today, after his second Wimbledon title, I know that Boris is at his best when he is despairing. He even has to be slightly hurt. It has to be raining, the hotel room mustn't be too comfortable – medium-class to shabby. Chicago is a great place for Boris. When he won there against Connors and Lendl, everything was dismal, grey and repulsive. He had a temperature, blood blisters on his feet and the hall was too hot, and old. In an atmosphere like this, his will asserts itself.

That was the mood we were in. Ion knocked on the door of the room. We were staying at the Gloucester; Boris had room 405, I had 406. It was half past eight, we were going for a meal. It was the night before the semi-finals. There had never been a seventeen-year-old in the semi-finals at Wimbledon before. Ion had found us a small Italian restaurant. There were just the three of us: Ion, Boris and I. Boris's parents, his sister Sabine and my wife had arrived in London, but were spending the evening without us. It was Ion's idea not to have anyone outside the team at the table the night before the match.

I won't go over what we talked about: it was too intimate and, in print, some things might

Mental training. Chess forms part of our pre-match preparations. We play through world championship games. Boris's favourite: power play, wham-bam, blow for blow

give the wrong impression. Of course, words cropped up like 'killer instinct', 'annihilate', 'run dead', 'killer forehand' and 'killer service'.

Outside, in the real world, Boris has never hit anyone. Even as a child, he wasn't one for a fight. Many times, I've seen him, in an argument with other kids, just turn round and walk away.

Tennis isn't like real life 'out there': it too is a fight for survival – but in tennis, there is the wonderful rule that opponents never touch one another.

We talked a mixture of English, German and Romanian. Since I don't speak English well, nor Ion German, and Boris only knows a little Romanian, our talk was reduced to a minimum, all the padding fell away, much of it sounded hard, non-committal.

During the meal, our mood was one of unshakeable optimism and defiance. The worst that could happen was defeat, 'death'. Or some-

thing like that. Jarryd, number six in the world, was Goliath, and Boris David. In that mood, we went back to the hotel: we were not afraid.

What fascinates me about Boris is that he can shake off pressure between one second and the next, just forget it. In Melbourne, the three of us were again coming back from a meal. Boris saw some scaffolding on a house. He pulled himself

up. 'Hey, how many pull-ups can you two do with one arm?' Boris did eight, I managed three, with Ion, in his suit, laughing at us. Now, in London too, Boris noticed everything: a drunk on the other side of the street, a funny car, a nice house-front, the moon scudding through the clouds ... Yes, things like that.

My wife always says Boris is a poet.

Out hotel was besieged by journalists; we went in by the back door. I could tell by the way Boris moved that he was itching to meet Jarryd the next day. Before a match, players like Boris radiate a strange kind of feeling: a kind of delirium or trance. Their body temperature is up, their brain feverish. It would be easy for an outsider to misread their body language, because they yawn, look tired, their movements are slow.

Yawning, Boris opened the door to his room.

I was feeling good.

The next day began well; the semi-finals were in the afternoon. Boris wasn't brooding, no serious thinking, but he seemed to be very alert. At breakfast, he had eaten well: two bowls of muesli, two plates of fruit. At about eleven o'clock, we went training. As I hit him the first few balls, Boris said, 'The feeling isn't there.' He often says that before matches. 'The feeling isn't there.' I ignored him.

'Never mind, just keep on playing. It'll be there.' The training session was terrible; he hardly hit the ball at all.

Sometimes he tries to play 'without any feelings', trying to get all the bad things out of him and go 'clean' onto the court.

Sometimes, it's also due to fear: 'Oh, I mustn't be too good. If I'm too good, I'll come over too strong.'

Previous page: *Boris is never alone: there's always someone watching, whether at training sessions or matches. This was in Australia, practising forehand volleys, for two hours solid*

And sometimes the feeling really isn't there – as if you could go to sleep on Earth one night and wake up the next morning on the dark side of the Moon. You get panicky.

What does it mean: 'The feeling's not there'?

It means you're there on court, playing, but you're not yourself. Someone else has taken over your body – someone clumsy, someone gauche. You haven't any feeling for the racket, no sense of rhythm, no feeling for the ball. That may sound eerie, but that's how it is in tennis.

It wasn't Boris playing the first set against Jarryd. Nothing went right for him, he was completely out of the game. Jarryd, on the other hand, played perfect tennis, one hard return after another. Almost effortlessly, Jarryd broke his service twice; he lost the set 2-6.

The second set started the same way as the first. His forehand wouldn't come, his backhand wouldn't come, his first service wouldn't come. Again and again, he gave me a look which said, 'The feeling isn't there, it just isn't there'. Between games, he covered his face with his towel. I could feel his desperate searching in my head.

He changed rackets. Five minutes later, he changed rackets again. He signalled, 'No feeling'. I ignored his signals. I had as little idea of what to do as he had – but I didn't dare show it. I had refused to accept his 'lack of feeling' since the first few shots in the training session.

'Keep playing,' I signalled to him. 'Just play, will you?' There was only one answer: keep playing.

He was in great danger. It looked as though the second set, too, was lost.

And then the incredible happened: at the moment of greatest danger, his feeling came back. At 4-5 and 30-40 – i.e. set point for Jarryd – Boris managed his first ace after 74 minutes. A second set-point was averted with an amazing volley. Then both players lost their service. Tie-break. Immediately, Boris was 1-3 down – but the feeling stayed with him, didn't leave him. He pulled back, hit two aces, two brutal returns. 7-3, set to Boris.

The sky grew dark. 1-all in the third set. Rain. The players waited. The rain teemed down. 'Rain stopped play', for the third time. It was

When you're a finalist at Wimbledon, you don't have to carry your gear on to court yourself. The man in the white coat does it for you – he's the changing-room manager. Here, in 1985, he acts as porter for Boris and Kevin Curren

7 p.m. We left the court as if drugged. Once more uncertainty, once more nothing had been settled.

But that wasn't the worst thing. The worst thing was playing without the feeling being there. What if it wasn't there again tomorrow?

Meanwhile, we had learnt who would be in the Finals: Kevin Curren. He'd knocked McEnroe out of the tournament. We didn't dare think about Curren. We had to think of Jarryd.

That night, I couldn't sleep. What was the matter with Boris? He doesn't forget bad matches. He goes over every point lost again and again. That was how he was now. Had the spectre of 'unfeelingness' got him in its grip?

The next day, Boris wiped Jarryd off the court 6-3, 6-3. It was as though Jarryd was in a daze: five times, Boris broke him, shot his fist heavenwards. He was the youngest finalist, the first unseeded player ever to reach the Finals at Wimbledon.

Today, I wonder how a seventeen-year-old could have stood all this. In fact, his strength should have been exhausted. There had been too many threatening situations by the time of the Finals. Already, Boris had been as good as dead against Nystrom. In the last set, it had been 5-4 to Nystrom – with him to serve at 30-all. All Nystrom needed was two points, and Boris would have been out. Boris survived two match points and went on to win the set 9-7.

I like Boris to weigh himself before a match. I want to know how much weight he loses during it. In the match against Nystrom, he went on court at 182 lbs and came off it at 173. We can make up the loss with vitamins, mineral drinks and a specially-tailored diet. But what about the nervous losses? You can't measure those. After matches like that against Nystrom – which lasted nearly four hours – Boris sits in the changing room and holds his head. His head hurts him more than his legs, arms or feet. Usually he goes to sleep on the massage table, exhausted by the mental effort.

One detail sticks out. Of course, Boris was insane with joy that he had reached the Finals. He hugged Ion and me, and if he was high. But he wasn't surprised – no, he really wasn't surprised. That showed me that reaching the Finals wasn't something real for him, but was like something in a dream. Nothing that happens in a dream is surprising.

There was no time to analyse Curren's game (he was number eight in the world at the time), or clue Boris in on him, or find a sparring partner who played the way he did. On Saturday afternoon, Boris was definitely in the Final. The Final was set for Sunday. Curren, ten years Boris's senior, had knocked Stefan Edberg, John McEnroe and Jimmy Connors out of the tournament, in straight sets each time. That said it all. Kevin was born in South Africa. When he's not playing tennis, he lives on his farm in Texas. He breeds cattle. He's quiet, gaunt, tall, controlled – personally, I like him a lot. What was I supposed to tell Boris about Kevin? He was a man.

That evening, we went for a meal: Ion, Boris and I. Boris's grandfather had died three days earlier. Ion and I had had a short talk together and, with the agreement of Boris's parents, had decided not to tell him. Nor did Boris know what was in the papers. The English press had headlines like 'Grenade-thrower', 'Bombardier', 'One man tank corps'; we kept these out of his sight, along with all the fuss in Germany. Ion was protecting us. Nor were we interested in the world outside. Boris never asked what the papers were saying. He had no idea that by now there were millions of Germans sitting in front of their TV sets, that Leimen was inundated with reporters. Who was Boris? What did he eat, what made him laugh, how did he live?

Boris's face was fuller then. Looking at it today, it's not the same any more. What a difference a year makes! In my memory, his face on the evening before the Final was soft, the skin slightly pink, rosy and excited, especially at the cheekbones. His temperature was up, as always. I remember how he stuck out his chin.

The evening before the Final was pleasant and calm. Ion talked about when he was a Davis Cup player. He made us laugh a lot.

Ion has been involved in just about everything in tennis. Once, in the Finals of the Davis Cup against the United States, he conducted the Romanian audience's singing with his racket as baton.

On the way back to the Gloucester Hotel, I noticed Boris was practising his hand movements. Forehand, backhand. His serving shoulder moved rhythmically. He was already playing.

His rackets were in his room. He will use eight during a tournament, and get through 100 in a year. They are much sought after as souvenirs, some are auctioned at charity events. The evening before a match, he is obsessed with his rackets. I carried a tensioning machine with me; it was in my room. I wouldn't let Boris's rackets be tensioned by the tournament service; I did it myself. I arranged it so he would have his rackets right there on the afternoon. When I first became his trainer, I wasn't allowed to touch his rackets. Only when he trusted me did he let me handle them. For him, rackets are like friends, a part of himself. Before a match, this feeling increases. He wants them near him; he holds them, plucks them, listens to the strings. The palm of his right (service) hand has a layer of calluses a centimetre thick. The ball of his left thumb is also covered in calluses. That comes from testing the hardness of the strings.

During a match, he will hit his left hand with the racket continually, to test its hardness; feeling it, hearing it: hard strings make a high note.

Preparations before a match also include music, which he chooses himself. I have no say in that at all. Usually, he has 30 or 40 tapes with him: some that calm him down, others that get him going. A year ago, he used music from the *Rocky* films to get himself worked up (he's seen them all). It gets him going to see Rocky running around in training, running up hills in lead shoes. These are the pictures Boris sees. All the time, he has a racket in his hand, swings the racket and listens to the music. He has no idea which racket he will use the next day; in the warm-up sessions, he will suddenly pick one and say, 'That's the one'.

When I went to wake Boris the next morning, he was already awake. We met downstairs in the breakfast room.

'How did you sleep?'

'OK,' he said. 'I dreamt about the Duchess of Kent. She was congratulating me on winning.' It was enough to make you laugh. We both laughed.

But it was true: Boris had dreamt of winning. He was full of confidence. We spent the morning playing chess. Boris was black: black is his colour. He likes black jeans, black shirts, black jackets, black cars. We hardly spoke during the game. Boris won. I wasn't trying too hard; I was happy for him to win. At that moment, every positive feeling was important. We gave up at 11 a.m. The car to take us to Wimbledon was due at 11.15.

His warming-up partner was the Czech, Slozil. After an hour, I stopped the warm-up session. Boris's shirt was soaked. I had deliberately made the session a hard one: Boris has such a slow pulse rate that I have to warm him up. Shower, massage, absolute quiet. Boris dozed. An hour later, we began on the stretching exercises.

To judge Boris by the state of his hotel room, you'd think he was an anarchist: it looks like a jungle. But when it comes to preparing for a match, he is a strict disciplinarian. He doesn't mess about. I'm there but I needn't be. He went through a complete stretching routine. To calm myself down, I went through most of it with him.

Each player prepares himself in a different way. Connors talks to himself, shouts at himself. McEnroe simmers quietly. Lendl talks and talks, he talks everyone into the ground – his masseur, his opponent. He tries to show himself how laid back he is. Boris is very quiet. Curren the same.

In the changing rooms, neither of them looked at the other; each one was on his own. In the changing rooms there was a colour monitor showing what was happening on the Centre Court. Since nothing much was going on, except for celebrities arriving in the Royal Box, a clock had been blended in. The second hand was moving soundlessly.

I was looking through the day's papers. *Tennis Magazine* wrote: 'The day Boris Becker stepped up for the Finals, there were 14,433 people in the stands at Wimbledon, nearly eleven million Germans and several hundred million people all round the world in front of their televisions ... The cool guy from Texas, a perfect example of self-control ... Boris, on the other hand, a temperament not yet fully harnessed. We couldn't believe our eyes: here, in the Final, he made a football shot *à la* Beckenbauer, bounced the ball a few times, and then gently kicked it to the ball-boy. Because that was the way he felt in that playful moment. That gives an idea of the boy from Leimen's legendary urge to play. Give him a ball, and he'll work magic with it, wherever he is.'

A few lines on, I read, 'Boris Becker's repertoire is polished ... Boris positions himself according to the state of the battle. Immediately, he was up at the net, with a very risky volley to the far corner. Overhead, he is in control, his opponent stands there in amazement. He produces dream balls out of the most unlikely situations; on the net, overreaching, a gentle cross which falls to the ground in front of his opponent. His game revels in the risky shot ...'

I think the millions of people who were seeing Boris for the first time were impressed above all by his commitment. Does commitment come under 'sacrifice'? Is that possible? His game is not just a matter of hitting the ball left or right, or bashing out his serves. Boris lives the game because he doesn't see it as a game, but as life. I've already said that he is not a laughing player, but a happy player. He likes building up a sweat. He likes the marks of battle on his body: the grazes from his falls – again and again after the Final he would show me his grazed right knee like a trophy, three inches of raw flesh. 'Look, Guntzi, look ...'

I have known many gifted athletes whose nerve broke when it came to the crunch, irrespective of how old or experienced they were. What is special about Boris is that his lust for battle is stronger than the fear in his stomach. He just can't imagine losing before a match. He just can't picture it. That is an incredible gift, in-born. You can't train for it. I can see that he is impatient and raring for the fight by the way he holds his neckchain, a gift from his mother, between his lips when he goes out: his teeth on it show the tension in his neck.

Is that a child or an adult going on to court? Both. I think his opponents couldn't cope when he appeared. What sort of a strange mixture was this coming on court? A seventeen-year-old, not even seeded. During the tournament, Boris had of course shown the emotions of a non-adult. Frequently, he really *was* only seventeen. After mishitting balls, he would whimper, 'I can't go on.' His red-blond hair, his 'baby face', his boyish, as yet not fully trained body, his face – never yet shaved. And then, the next minute: bang, bang, bang came his serves. A shock for his opponent.

Curren played the way I'd feared: hard and tough. But Boris beat him down in his initial spurt and broke his service straight away. A magical set: 6-3.

The winning ball. A cry to heaven; fists clenched. Seventeen years old. Curren has lost. Victory at Wimbledon: the first

The minutes after the victory. You're in a daze. You can't sit back, stretch your legs, say, 'Man, I've won.' There's no time to think about what you've achieved. There's so much to be done: receive the cup from the Duke and Duchess of Kent, say a few words, do a lap of honour with the cup. As Boris kisses the trophy, a moment to himself

The winner at Wimbledon has his hands full: he carries the trophy, the MC carries his gear. Curren carries his bag himself. In the stands, Boris's parents hug each other. An hour later, all the Beckers are beaming: sister Sabine, mother Elvira, father Karl-Heinz and Boris with the trophy in front of the venerable clubhouse

That meant he wanted to know how things stood. Those are the kind of things I notice. I don't know if they make me feel any calmer.

The Final statistics (Boris still knows them by heart today):

Boris Becker–Kevin Curren
6-3, 6-7 (4-7), 7-6 (7-3), 6-4.
Wimbledon, 7 July 1985.
Duration of match: 3 hours 17 minutes.

	Becker	Curren
First service in court	61%	48%
Baseline faults	20	15
Net faults	10	21
Double faults	7	8
Break points	17	6
Breaks	3	1
Direct points		
Aces	21	19
Service	36	42
Forehand	2	3
Backhand	1	1
Passing shots (forehand)	8	3
Passing shots (backhand)	3	5
Volleys	27	12
Smashes	8	3
Returns	16	11
Lobs	0	1
Drops	0	0
Total points		
Own score	124	80
Through opponent's faults	44	37
Total	148	117

In the second set, Curren didn't yield an inch. 6-all, tie-break. Curren hammered five points out of Boris, one after another.

Those five points hammered in my brain.

1-all. One set each. Boris wiped his towel across his face. His feet were wobbling. He still held his racket. I always tell him, 'As long as you've still got your racket in your hand, you haven't lost.'

He had his racket in his hand. That's the sort of thing I noticed. Did it make me feel any calmer? I don't know. My hands were cold.

'Time!' the umpire called. Boris got up first.

Was I afraid? Doubting? I don't know. We were flying through a dream. Three hours and seventeen minutes the Final lasted. The pictures show me jumping up, waving my fists – like Boris on the court. Ion stayed sitting down next to me. Of 14,433 spectators, he was the only one who stayed sitting down. At his feet were the cigarette ends from three packets. After the game was over – I never realized it until now – we would never be the same again. No one in the team would.

ION TIRIAC

Three years ago, our life was … well, things get blurred in memory. Boris, my wife and I had recently been for a meal at the Château Eza, up in the mountains, 30 minutes by car from Monte Carlo. It was once the holiday residence of the kings of Sweden. Today it's a hotel and restaurant, famous for its views over the Côte d'Azur – you can see as far as Villefranche – and for its fillet steak, which they wrap up in whisper-thin gold leaf.

Boris was taking us out. We were celebrating his second win at Wimbledon. 'You eat the gold leaf as well,' the chef de cuisine told us. 'That 's how the kings of France ate their meat.'

'I hope it doesn't rustle when you chew it,' said Boris. We collapsed laughing, and the chef de cuisine turned away, offended.

It was a beautiful evening, below us we could see the lights of Villefranche sparkling. Boris said, 'We lived down there once.'

A modest bedsitter in Villefranche – the way we lived three years ago. The rooms were so small, you opened the door and fell over the bed. We were getting ready for the Monte Carlo youth tournament. Boris was sixteen. We went shopping in supermarkets, ate sandwiches in our room at night …

How Ion Tiriac likes to see himself – at the top. Not surprising, since he came from the bottom. His mother sold vegetables on the street. Ion fought his way up – by using his talent and his head

My God, that wasn't even three years ago.

It was at that time that I first showed Boris to Ion Tiriac. I'd already told him about Boris. Although we had gone our different ways after I had defected from Romania, Ion and I had always kept in touch. We would either meet at tournaments or phone. Again and again, Ion would say, 'I don't understand you Germans. You make the best cars, play good football – why haven't you got any tennis players? Tell me if you find one. You're the youth trainer; you're bound to see them.'

A year before, I had hinted to him, 'I've found one, but give me a bit more time.'

Now at the Monte Carlo tournament, I told Ion, 'Take a look at Boris. He's still a bit crazy. He may lose a dead-cert match now and then. He's crazy. He can never forget his mistakes … But take a look at him for yourself.'

Ion sat down next to me. As always, there was no expression on his face. He didn't say a word the whole match.

Wojtek Fibak, a very good Polish player, once said of Ion, 'No one has ever seen his teeth.' He meant that Ion never smiled. I know the other Ion. Of course he smiles.

Ilie Nastase, who knows Ion as well as I do – he was his doubles partner for many years – summed him up better: 'Ion likes to play the cool guy, get people worried, make them think he's a tough nut. He acts the same way with his son: hard and tough when other people are around, but soft as a kitten when they're alone.'

When Boris had finished, and won the match, Ion said, 'Vilas should test him.'

Guillermo Vilas had been Ion's pupil for many years. After Borg and Bergelin, they were the most impressive partnership in the history of tennis. With Ion as coach and partner, Vilas got to number two in the world, setting an amazing record – 50 singles wins in succession. Vilas won the French, American and Australian championships. Ion led Vilas safely through the maze of international tennis.

I can't haggle over contracts or sing people's praises as if they were gods. I'm no businessman. We needed a man like Ion.

Let me explain.

At that time, three or four years ago, I was travelling the world with my group of four. I've already mentioned the boys: there was Udo Riglewski, Patrick Kühnen, Karl Uwe Steeb and Boris. My idea was to go through all the hurdles with the four of them: by 'hurdles' I mean dragging yourself through the qualifying rounds in the men's tournaments. I told the boys, 'Anyone who qualifies gets a wild card for the next tournament.' A wild card gets you automatically into the main field; only then do you have a chance of getting world ranking points.

Wild cards are given out by the associations or tournaments. It's almost unbelievable: 90 tennis players travel to a tournament, they all have to go through the qualifying rounds, but only 32 can make it. Most of them arrive with rucksacks and sleeping-bags, and sleep in the changing-rooms. As I've said, we met Stefan Edberg – now in the top five in the world – rolled up in a sleeping-bag in a changing cubicle.

Generally, you only see the lives of those at the top: Boris, Lendl, McEnroe ... but down there, where it all comes together, it's a fight for survival.

Once, we were travelling to a tournament in Vienna. I'd promised Boris a wild card – he'd earned it. He was by far the best in my group. But there was no wild card there for him. He travelled all that way, skipped school – all for nothing.

I said to the General Secretary of the Austrian Association: 'If you give Boris one, an Austrian youngster will get two wild cards for German tournaments.'

I had to put it in writing. But I didn't have the DTB's backing. That's the sort of trick I used to get Boris world points. The DTB people would have turned me down flat. I was lying through my teeth.

As I came into the DTB's sports director's office, he was already grumbling, 'Don't keep on at me about Becker. We don't need any extras.'

Face to face with them, I was quite humble. 'But he has an extraordinary talent. He deserves a wild card.'

'Not a chance, not a chance.'

Every time I opened the door it was the same: 'Not Becker again. I'm fed up with hearing that name.'

We both depended on the DTB for our livelihoods – I as a trainer, Boris as a player. Because I had included Boris in my quartet, he had a training contract with the DTB. The Association had undertaken to cover flights, accommodation and subsistence. If Boris later started to win prizes, the money would be divided in a given ratio between Boris and the DTB. That sounds good, but really it was just one long, miserable struggle. 'Bosch,' they told me, 'You've got Becker on the brain.'

I wasn't up to these battles any more. I had already thought of Ion a year before Monte Carlo. What we needed was a manager, an experienced tennis and finance man who understood us. Boris had to play against the best. The best played in America, Australia, London, Tokyo and Paris. Playing the best meant flying, living in hotels; it meant money.

200,000 marks a year – without having to feel bad about it. We needed someone who would simply dare to invest that amount. We needed someone who believed in Boris. Ion. We needed someone like Ion.

But all I got from the DTB was, 'Bosch, you've got Becker on the brain.'

Yes – I have, I still do. In my whole life, I had only come across one young player like Boris: Ilie Nastase. At that time, I was his youth trainer in Romania. Nastase and Boris are two completely different players. But when I saw Boris again after the trials in Biberach (the ones where he failed), it was like a case of *déjà vu*.

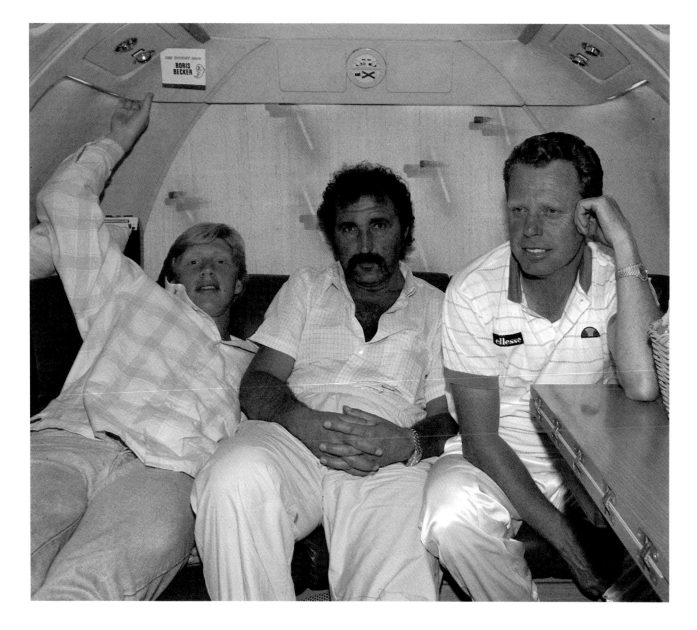

In a Lear jet from Cincinnati to the Johnny Carson Show in Los Angeles. The only one afraid of flying is the passenger in the middle with the folded hands

Players like Nastase, Connors or Borg are like members of a single species. They have something others don't. And Boris has it too. Did Boris's parents also think I was mad?

Basically, I was fighting on two fronts: the DTB front and the Leimen front. Boris's mother was determined that he shouldn't neglect his schoolwork. Boris was in the fifth form at the Helmholtz Gymnasium (grammar school). He ought to take O-levels at least; but his mother would have been happiest if we could have combined tennis and school: tennis and A-levels. From her point of view, she was right. There is nothing more uncertain than a professional career. What if it goes wrong? Then you have a kid of twenty-two with no career and no proper education.

But you can only do one thing. Boris would certainly have passed his A-levels; perhaps not as top of the class, because even as a semi-professional he would have had to have trained, but he would have done it. He always managed somehow. He has a photographic memory. He would read pages from his biology book in the evening and write them out in class the next morning from memory. He would have got through.

But half-measures don't work.

So those were the fronts. At the DTB, I was fighting for money, with his parents I was fighting for his tennis future; and in my head was Ion.

The discussions with Boris's parents were important for all of us. Boris could never have turned out the way he did without his parents pulling with us. Boris and I could live with the solution the school board finally came up with. (The idea went like this: Boris would leave school after O-levels, drop it for two years and then go back to school if tennis didn't work out. They would keep a place open for him, so to speak.)

After the match in Monte Carlo had finished, Ion said, 'I'd like Vilas to train with him. Is tomorrow OK?' No: by that time, Boris would already be back at his school desk.

We agreed that the trials with Vilas would take place during the German championships at Rothenbaum in Hamburg. Vilas had entered, and so had Boris.

Ion and I went down to meet Boris.

How can I describe their first meeting? At that time, Boris was very timid. Of course, he was impressed by the name Ion Tiriac – Vilas was one of his idols – but even more by Ion's appearance, his drooping moustache, his dark eyes, the 'overgrown' face, dominated by his eagle's nose.

I acted as interpreter: Boris couldn't speak English like he can now, and Ion had forgotten his school German.

So we left and met again in Hamburg. The test had been arranged. I was keen to see what would

Not many people can remember Ion without his moustache. I met him at fifteen, when I showed him how to play tennis. Ion without his moustache was exactly like Ion with his moustache: thick-skulled, obsessed, hard-working

happen. Never before had Boris played against a world-class player like Vilas (I think he was number five in the world at the time). Now we would see if he was up to it.

We looked for a quiet spot where there were no spectators.

Vilas is a player who can play back and forth endlessly for hours. That's not exactly the sort of tennis I like; but it is athletic tennis which goes right to the heart of the matter. Vilas can take another player apart because he himself makes very few mistakes.

They played each other for five hours, interrupted only by Ion's directions to Vilas, changes of ends, discussions about individual strokes. They went through it all: hard match training, several sets. Vilas is a player who keeps the rally going. Right, left and again and again at Boris's backhand, which of course at that time was still developing. Ion and I took turns as umpire.

After the quality of play, the main question was how Boris would come through the heights and depths of such a trial. Vilas was quite clearly better than him. Boris was fifteen, Vilas thirty. Vilas had thousands of battles behind him, innumerable finals against Borg and McEnroe. It was a question of how Boris would act when the chips were down: when he couldn't run any more because his muscles were clogged up, when only his will was driving him on. Ion wanted to see how self-sacrificing Boris was, what his weak points were. Only when you're 'dead' in tennis does your character show.

I don't know whether I've said it already: Ion is obsessed with tennis – but money rules the world. And Ion is someone who doesn't like being wrong. If he says 'Yes' to a player, he likes to be right for his own sake (his image?). Ion is really two people: coolly calculating on the one hand and imaginative on the other. Ion is someone who knows how to dream. Sometimes I think he doesn't care about money, but only about realizing his dream: 'I'm right.'

Later, we (Boris, Ion and I) would have terrible rows about how we would make his (Ion's) and our dream come true. Ion was hitting his head against a brick wall; but so was Boris. Ion had never taken my word for it – 'Here is Boris, the greatest.' Ion wanted to see for himself. That was OK, too.

During the trial, Boris hurt his shoulder. His service, with which he was holding off Vilas's power, wouldn't work any longer.

'Shall we go on?' Ion asked me. Neither he nor Vilas knew Boris. In St Anton, Boris had been ill during a run against adults up a steep hill. They had all given up – he was a child, running against men – but he wouldn't give up. As he passed the finishing line, he had to be sick.

I wanted to see for myself how far Boris would go. I wanted to see if he had it in him. It was

Vilas or him. It wasn't Boris who threw in the towel after five hours. Vilas asked us, 'Seen enough?'

I can still see Vilas's figure today. He was wearing this headband, his hair was plastered to his head, his lungs were hammering against his chest. Boris was squatting down, his racket between his legs. Boris was near to collapse; but he had kept on playing.

'Günther,' said Ion, 'we must talk to his parents. Can you make an appointment?'

I spoke with Boris's parents and rang Ion in Paris: 'Come.'

The idea that Ion arrived in Leimen in a Rolls is something the press dreamed up. We (Boris, his parents, Ion and I) met at the airport hotel in Frankfurt. Ion came by scheduled flight from Paris, we came by car. Ion had hired a day suite. In these rooms, we sat and talked.

Of course, things didn't happen as fast as they appear here. Two or three weeks passed between the Hamburg trial and our meeting in Frankfurt. Evening after evening, I sat with the Beckers in Leimen.

Who was Ion Tiriac anyway? Boris and his father knew, but not Frau Becker. All that she had heard sounded very exotic in their living-room in Leimen. Apartments in Paris, New York, Monte Carlo. Tennis facilities in Paris and on Long Island.

'Is he married?'

'No, divorced.'

'Is he a refugee from Romania like you, Herr Bosch?'

'No, he's a Romanian living abroad: a Romanian citizen officially allowed to live in the West.'

'But they're Communists over there.'

'Ion Tiriac has special status. He's done a lot for Romania as a sports star and manager.'

'Is he living with a woman?'

'No, he lives with his son and his sister.'

'Where does he get his money from?'

'He's a manager. He marketed Vilas like no other tennis star has ever been marketed before.'

'Herr Bosch, is he trustworthy? There was this scandal ...'

Father and son. For me, this is my favourite
picture of them. Karl-Heinz Becker, Boris's
father, is a pretty good tennis player himself. The
first racket Boris ever picked up was one of his
father's. His sister showed him how to hold it.
She is training to be an architect – like her father

The Beckers meant the 60,000-dollar starting fee Vilas was supposed to have been paid by Rotterdam tournament officials. Vilas had been barred for a year.

'He was acquitted on appeal,' I said. 'The first hearing was a farce.'

Boris's mother: 'Well, I don't know, Herr Bosch ...'

I said, 'Ion Tiriac is the best.'

Boris's mother said, 'Shouldn't we talk with ProServ or the people from McCormack?'

ProServ and McCormack are the two biggest sports agencies. Their scouts, who never miss a tournament, had brought Boris to their attention. Boris's parents had been made offers guaranteeing him hundreds of thousands of marks a year.

This was the mood when we met in Frankfurt. Boris wasn't interested in what we were talking about. He paced back and forth in the suite, looking out of the window. What a lot of talk ... Those were his words. Boris can't sit in a room for four or five hours: he just wants to be outside.

Ion threw me. He said, 'Please, Günther, tell the Becker family I can't guarantee a kid anything. Tell them I'm not mad. Tell them I can't guarantee the kid a penny.'

I translated what he said.

Ion: 'Please tell them also that their son has potential. I'll try and develop it. Tell them I'll finance his tournament schedule for two years.'

I translated.

'Can I say something else?' Ion asked me. I nodded. 'Tell them Boris can play with you anywhere, never mind where. Tell them I'll fund both of you for just two years, not a day longer.' It was fantastic. No one was talking about money. No one wanted Boris to earn money fast. Everyone wanted him to learn. That's how we became a team: Ion, Boris – and me.

We went to the DTB office in Hanover. That's Ion: can't wait one single day, then or ever. We had to buy Boris and myself out of our DTB contracts.

'How much?' asked Ion.

'Twenty thousand marks,' they said at the DTB. I'll never forget the scene. Ion reached into his inside pocket. He was going to put down the 20,000 marks in cash. The DTB people were embarrassed. 'Can't we set it off against the Davis Cup? If Boris plays against Spain at Sindelfingen, we're quits.'

Then we sorted out who would meet the costs of Wimbledon a few weeks later (he would win it the year after ...). Wimbledon was on Boris's old DTB schedule.

'OK, OK, we'll pay for Wimbledon,' said the DTB people.

Just for the record, I must point out that Ion offered the DTB a share in his funding schedule for the next two years. They turned it down.

They accepted my resignation immediately. We were free.

As it happened, I'd built a terrace house just outside Hanover, with a little capital of my own and the rest under a mortgage.

'Bosch, you're crazy, you're giving up a job for life,' said my friends. They didn't know I would also be getting less money with Tiriac.

'If it doesn't work out, we'll sell the house,' my wife said. I only put this down to give some idea of the sort of adventure we were letting ourselves in for.

Boris and I travelled to Wimbledon at the DTB's expense. We arrived in London and gave the taxi-driver the address of the hotel where the DTB had booked rooms for us.

Simple, modest – we weren't bothered, we were used to it. The hotel *was* simple and modest, but also very noisy. The rooms were rented by the hour. Through the thin walls, we could hear who came and who went. We'd ended up in a brothel! That was the last trip (but one) the DTB ever paid for.

Overleaf: *Finalists' celebration dinner at the Savoy, 1985. Boris holds the Wimbledon trophy, and we look on. I'm the only one without a dinner jacket: I didn't order one before the match out of superstition – and by then it was too late*

DEFEATS
AND OTHER UPSETS

Two and a half years of Boris! Day after day: even when we had a week's holiday after his second win at Wimbledon, we hung around together.

It is Saturday in Monte Carlo and very hot. I'm working on this book under a parasol in the Sea Club at the Beach Plaza Hotel. I'm thinking about our defeats; we don't always win. I'm dictating my thoughts on to tape. Boris is lying in the blazing sun.

'Hey, get in the shade or put something on!' I call to him.

Boris is currently trying to convince himself he's a sun-lover. 'I love the sun,' he says. 'Look how brown I'm getting.'

In Johannesburg, 2000 metres up, he tried to convince me in all seriousness that he liked playing best at midday. But what happened? He got heatstroke, had a temperature and the shivers. That was two years ago. 'Look, how many times have I told you – put your hat on, put your hat on.'

Boris: 'Out there, I won't be playing with my hat on.'

Ninety seconds: then the player must get back on court. Boris, lost, changing ends against Nystrom in Flushing Meadow, 1986. All his gear is in a heap: rackets, sweatbands, towels. Defeat stares him in the face

Ten minutes later, Boris comes under the parasol, his face red. He turns his face away. With his light skin, intense sunlight is a problem; it makes playing difficult for him. If he can't keep his eyes properly open and he runs around squinting in the harsh light, his strokes go wild and he misses the ball. In Australia and Johannesburg, he hit balls right over the stands.

Boris is watching me. 'Haven't you finished that book yet? How far have you got?'

'With the ups and downs, your crack-up last year.'

Boris puts his feet on the table, a hero in the sun.

'But it didn't happen. Have you read what they're writing now? "Boris the riddle, the secret Boris ... How did he cope with winning in 1985? With all the defeats afterwards, the millions he's earned since." Come on, we'll do the chapter together.'

Boris was alight; we talked for two hours. The tape was running. Boris asked me questions, and I asked him some.

Boris: 'Everyone had predicted disaster. Psychologists, everyone, in America or Germany. Shows you how much idea they have ... The statements kept coming the whole year: seventeen, it's too early, he'll break down. It'll end in tears. The millions will be the end of him. He doesn't laugh as much as he used to...'

Me: 'Sometimes you really flipped; there were matches – Schapers, Nystrom...'

Boris: 'Yes, but those writers don't know me at

Winning and losing shows on Boris's face – but not on Nystrom's. They played each other twice in a week: at the semi-finals in Cincinnati, Nystrom lost; at Flushing Meadow, he won. His face doesn't change. He was born near the North Pole; perhaps that has something to do with it

Previous page: *The winner at Cincinnati, by the hotel pool. Life is good: sun, deckchair, Walkman, sunglasses. I thought he had 20 pairs of sunglasses; he says he's only got 10*

all. I cracked up because I can't forget mistakes. In the match against Wilkison in Atlanta, when I had the chance to score a point with my forehand, and I missed it – I flipped out. I couldn't forget that screwed-up forehand. OK, I went mad.'

Me: 'And you lost the march, stamped your feet like a little kid whose mother wouldn't give him any chocolate.'

Boris: 'You never forget anything, do you?' … OK, OK, afterwards, I thought: is something wrong with you? Why are you cracking up like this? And then, next day, the papers … again and again, I could read between the lines: "Wimbledon I was pure chance, luck …" Although I've shown I can play – beaten Lendl, beaten Wilander, won all my Davis Cup matches under maximum pressure, won in Munich, in Germany, in Cincinnati … When we were in Düsseldorf two

months ago, playing exhibition matches, these two psychologists came to our hotel ... You listened to them ... I hated you for that, I can't tell you how much ... They can plant codes in your brain, alarm clocks ... What a lot of rubbish! What did they actually say?'

Me: 'They came from the Cologne Sports College. They said they trained athletes' unconscious minds. They quoted deadline pressure as an example. You know: you come home late, you've got an important appointment next day, you have to get up at six, the plane leaves at seven. In a case like that, your "internal alarm" would wake you up. That's what they're doing with athletes they said, even a few tennis players.'

Boris: 'Which ones?'

Me: 'They didn't mention any names – district leagues, associations.'

Boris: 'Am I playing in a district league?'

At this point I'd like to break off our conversation for a minute. Of course, things looked bad when Boris cracked up, lost himself in self-recrimination and wailed up at me. 'Boris is broken for good', the headlines read. One paper wrote: 'On court, he behaves like a child tearing the leg off its doll.' On the other hand, when he was at his most desperate, he got up off the ground and hit his best shots. Psychologists, experts of all kinds, rang us up, offered to travel as part of our team. Thirty of them alone spoke with his parents. I listened to some of them – after all, some of them were scientists who had to be taken seriously – but I wouldn't let any of them near Boris. The question the three of us (Boris, Ion and myself) faced was: How can Boris keep his head without us changing his soul, his ego? It wasn't Wilkison, Dyke or Schapers who had beaten Boris. Boris had beaten himself.

Boris asked us, 'Well, aren't I allowed to lose?' We replied, 'Yes, but not that way.' Ion and I spent many nights talking. Ion had Vilas as the model in his head. But Boris is not Vilas. With Vilas, Ion had the advantage of being able to operate a 'machine'. Vilas reacted 100 per cent to Ion's signals and push-buttons. There were no 'no's' or 'buts' or doubts of any kind. What Ion told Vilas to do, he did – and they achieved success. But Boris is not Vilas, you can't operate him on remote control – 'Watch your forehand. Attack. Play the volley across court...'

I'm all in favour of trainers helping during matches, but that mustn't lead to control being taken from the player. With Boris, the main thing is he can play vital shots when he's on the ground. There has to be some room to man-oeuvre – my players must develop their own creativity. When the chips are down, I can offer him my calmness and absolute loyalty – but I don't give him any orders. I give Boris hints. Boris is not obliged to accept them. (I'll go into more detail about our signs later.) Ion has gone through whole sequences with Vilas, and Vilas has carried them out. That can lead to some success, but not special, out-of-the-ordinary success.

But now there were these intrusions. Which 'school' was right? Mine or Ion's? And which school was right outside tennis?

Ion often accused me, 'Günther, you're too soft, you're not his father or mother, you're his trainer.'

I didn't know who was right. I didn't want to change Boris. My feelings told me that the right way had to come from Boris himself. I was rely-ing on his instincts.

I had never trained a world star, and Boris was new to the part himself. Boris the world star gets his daily schedule from Tiriac's manage-ment: 7 a.m. get up, 7.30 breakfast, 9.30 fly out, arrive in Washington, reception at German Embassy, press conference for UNICEF, 12.30 lunch at Hotel X with Ethel Kennedy, Foreign Secretary Schultz, General Haig, afternoon, tennis match at White House.

UNICEF, the UN children's relief organiza-tion, had made Boris a special ambassador, a role shared by Liv Ullman and Peter Ustinov. Boris put all his heart into it. Instead of playing in a 350,000-dollar tournament, he wanted to fly with UNICEF to Nicaragua, to show children there that injections were nothing to be afraid of. But the management said, 'Sorry, Boris, you have to play.'

We were on a zigzag course.

Who was I? Was I still a tennis coach? Who was he? Still a tennis player?

He beat Lendl and lost to a nobody. Boris was lost in the fog. I could hear him shouting (he didn't really shout, but I could feel it), 'Where am I? Am I an ambassador? A hero? Am I the player who beats Lendl more often than Lendl beats me?'

We had both started off thinking we were playing tennis; but then we saw the screaming teenagers, suddenly we had no time to ourselves any more. What can I do against an organization like Philips? Boris had to give 5000 autographs for Philips' business friends. He had to go on television. He had to be on 'Good Morning, America' at 6 a.m. on the dot – a programme seen coast-to-coast in the US.

Before, we could stroll around in any town. Today, we can't be alone anywhere on five conti-nents. If Boris leaves his hotel room, he meets people in the hallway who recognize him. The stares go on in the lift, it gets worse and worse, until he's surrounded in the foyer. Thirty feet from the hotel, he can't go another step. People grab hold of him.

US Foreign Secretary Schultz, UNICEF ambassador Becker and tennis star Vilas go begging at the UNICEF reception in Washington – for the children of the Third World

Sometimes I can see a certain pleasure in his eyes, sometimes panic.

Ion screened him off: it couldn't go on this way. We got bodyguards. The bodyguards accompanied us through back doors where limousines were waiting for us. We ate in reserved side rooms.

Only on the tennis court was Boris free – but here he was caving in. How do you train a world star?

In Atlanta, after the Wilkison defeat, Ion, Boris and I decided: hard training, no reporters, no TV pictures. We trained only for the WCT indoor championships in Dallas – six hours a day.

Suddenly, in a training session around midday, Boris turned away, pressed his hands against his forehead, took a few staggering steps like a drunk and leant against the wall of the indoor court, his face turned away from me.

I could see from his shoulders that he was crying.

I left him alone for a few minutes, picked the balls up, then came past where he stood. 'Don't be ashamed,' I said, 'let it out.'

We broke off the training session and went back to our hotel. I left him on his own for an hour; then I gave our special knock on his door. Boris opened it, radiant. All was forgotten. 'Guntzi, it's amazing, I've got rid of it, it's out!'

WCT world championships in Dallas. The top clan, with cowboy hats – without Lendl (injured), McEnroe (temporarily retired) and Connors (banned). Only Grand Slam winners and the best on points from the Super Series can take part at Dallas. Standing, left to right: Annacone, Kriek, Noah, Jarryd, Anger, Mecir. Seated: Gilbert, Edberg, Wilander, Nystrom, Boris, Tulasne

The rocky road: training at Crans-Montana (1500 metres up). A training session lasts three hours. We ran across the rough terrain, climbed walls, slalomed down forest slopes, ducked under branches, leapt over tree-trunks: all power and concentration exercises in the wild. In the afternoon, active relaxation with golf, in the evening, back to work again: basketball indoors, important for legwork

Overleaf: *Tracks in the snow: Boris at St Christina, Italy, on his Christmas holidays with his parents. Instead of jogging, cross-country skiing. He can also do downhill skiing and schuss; he skis well*

I thought I would find Boris desperate. How alone he must have been for a crying fit to make him happy again...

I can't talk to Ion about such things. Ion is giving us all the opportunities. He didn't care if we brought in money or not. Boris's success is Ion's success too. But Ion only knows Boris as a world star.

It all happened so fast. When I took Boris off his parents' hands, he was still running around with a name-tag on his chest so he wouldn't get lost. I picked him up at the airport. Boris couldn't shut a suitcase. He can now; and he can fold up his suits and put them in his suitcase. And when we arrive, that's the first thing he does: suitcase open, shake his jackets out and hang them up in the wardrobe. I help him a bit with the packing, always keeping an eye open to make sure he doesn't forget anything.

To be a world star – for Boris, that's priority number one: tennis. Everything else comes afterwards. And that's why I help him with his packing. Ion is someone who has built a barbed-wire fence around his heart, so to speak. Even in front of Boris, he plays the cold, hard super-manager. Coca-Cola, Philips, Deutsche Bank, Puma – he deals with them all...

Neither Boris nor I have any idea what one- or two-million-mark contracts mean. Boris has no idea what a million marks is.

We live on expense allowances.

A telephone in a hotel room – the link to home. Last year, we were in Germany for just fourteen days. Boris only phones home when he wins; if he loses, he leaves it. For Boris, the worst thing about living in hotels is the constant packing and unpacking: checking in, checking out. Tiriac Management reckons our travelling costs are 1.5 million marks a year

Entering the arena. Paris '86, sand court. The quarter-finals. Behind Boris, Pernfors. The players' faces are serious. They put their bags down, warm up for five minutes. Boris signals to Pernfors: give me a few balls to smash

Overleaf: *Against Wilander, Paris '85. A forehand volley on the run. In '86, Boris got through to the quarter-finals, in '85 he went out in the second round*

If Boris wants to buy a tape, he'll say to me, 'Give me five dollars.' I pass the invoice to Tiriac Management. When Boris was eighteen, he got a credit card. When he buys a suit, he gives me the counterfoil and I send it to his parents, who check it. Ion Tiriac is not the way he acts. I once told a reporter how touching and emotional Ion can be in private. Afterwards he growled at me, 'You're wrecking my image. My image is being hard.'

Like Boris, I'm new to this world. I answered Ion: 'For heaven's sake, does that count as image-wrecking? Is there no link between what you feel and what you say?'

Ion once said in an interview that Boris had grown up more in the last year than most people do in a hundred years.

I don't know about that.

Looked at from the outside, we look like the perfect team, us on the outside and Boris in the middle. There were times he seemed to me like a child whose parents were quarrelling. When we went for a meal, he would be between us, his arms around us. That was what last year was like.

In Paris, when he lost to Pernfors on the sand court, a few weeks before winning at Wimbledon for the second time, Boris found the right way from within himself. He talks about that time on tape.

'Paris, Pernfors, last set, 0-6 ... Guntzi, you said you'd never seen me lose like that ... with my hands up ... My parents were there. My father thought, "You didn't play that badly." To comfort me ... My mother was downstairs in the hotel. I left you on your own, went for a walk with her.

'Sister of the Year': Sabine Becker, 23, student, congratulates her brother on winning the 'Bambi' at Munich. Sabine still lives at home with her parents

That was the best moment in Paris, walking alone with her through the streets after losing to Pernfors ... I cracked up after the game too. In the changing-room, I beat my head against the wall. I was completely finished.

'This can't be real, I told myself. I feel really fantastic, walking through Paris with my mother, really relieved. I'd lost to Pernfors only that afternoon, but now I was happy with my mother. She didn't try to pick my brains. Then I asked myself, Why is it this way? Why can't I always feel like this? OK, I can't every day, but I thought: I can try – I have to try to enjoy life. I have to decide my own life. And, for the next few days, I did just what I felt like doing.

'I said I didn't want to see you or Ion.

'I thought about it ... OK, if I play well in a match, it works. But if I have a minor problem in the match, I cave in and can't help myself any more. I thought about why it was that way.

'It's this life. I'm living without any problems, I don't have to do anything for myself. Wherever I am – Paris, Rome, New York. My life's like a dream, no problems anywhere. But then – if a problem occurs on court, I can't deal with it. And I thought: Hey, why not get away from those two? Don't see them for two days. Now drive off somewhere and hide out, try and ring someone, get them to tow the car away. That sort of thing ... drive to the airport on your own and find your own way back

'They had told me not to drive in Paris. I simply pinched the car, drove to the airport. Followed the signs. I got there all right, but it took me hours to get back – it normally takes half an hour.

'I got into a jam. I'd never been on my own in a jam before. After two and a half hours, I got back to the hotel. I felt really fantastic!

'I'd been invited to a players' gala that evening. Someone had given me the address. I went off on my own, got lost, but I didn't ask anyone the way. I wanted to find it myself. After an hour and a half, I found the place. I felt as good as if I'd read a book – so much more complete, fulfilled.

'That sounds crazy, but it's the truth.

'While I was looking for the address, I suddenly ran out of petrol. I had to look for a petrol station. Of course, I could have told the hotel

porter, "Fill it up, I'll give you the money." He would have done it. I could also have said, "Drive me there." Anyone would have done it, but I wanted to do it on my own. And I did.'

(Me interrupting on the tape) 'Boris, driving in Paris is a problem. That's why Ion and I advised you against it. Just getting round the Arc de Triomphe is an art in itself. You've no driving experience. When you came to me and said, "I'm off", I really had my doubts. You took the car-keys. I hope nothing happens, I hope he doesn't write the car off, I thought. Two days you drove around in the car. I was afraid every minute. Then I took a look at the car. There wasn't a scratch on it.'

Boris: 'Even the gears. That's the first time I'd driven a car with a manual gearbox. For the first five minutes, I drove like you.'

That was the way, the way he won Wimbledon II.

Boris's outburst was not as mannerly as it sounds on tape. There was a lot of shouting, slamming of doors. 'That's it, I'm finished!'

Boris – and I am in a position to judge – is the best-looked-after player in the world. But he was also the most tied down. Our hotel in Paris was the feudal Royal Monceau, where the

With this shout after winning the match against Mecir (6-4, 6-2, 7-6), Boris lays the ghost of Wimbledon II. One more game, then he's in the Final. He's over the worst: getting to the semi-finals shows that Wimbledon I was no accident

Overleaf: *It's not often you see such relaxed faces after a semi-final at Wimbledon. For Leconte, it was a victory to get this far; for Boris, winning (6-2, 6-4, 6-7, 6-3) meant his second Final*

The Final. Lendl's forehand drives Boris well outside the court. **Centre:** *Boris pulls back for a backhand volley.* **Right:** *Lendl is beaten; the second after the winning shot*

furnishings have hardly changed since the time of the Sun King. So that Boris would not be distracted, we – Ion and I – were the only people he saw. We ate lunch together, dinner together – not even my wife or Ion's girlfriend was allowed along. That was Ion's creed: Boris had to concentrate, to do nothing but play, the management would take care of everything else. We trained in the hotel's own Viti tennis club ('Viti' stands for 'VItas' and 'TIriac'); no one else's car, no reporter got in without a special pass. We were mad. As I see it now, Boris put the brakes on just in time.

When Boris and I flew to London to get ready for Wimbledon, we found a four-man management reception committee waiting for us at Heathrow. We sent them away.

We loaded our luggage and bags – eighteen pieces of luggage in all – into taxis. Both Boris and I put our backs into it.

During the Wimbledon warm-up weeks at Queens, we trained in the same courts as everyone else, used the same tournament cars as the number 300 in the world – no more special treatment.

Ion gave us a free hand.

We were back with the pack again.

Boris on tape again: 'You have to live with the pack, Guntzi ... Do you remember the last ball but one in the Final against Lendl – that drop shot? If you were soft, you'd let it go. But if you're a wolf, you want it. I was in full stride, when the net changed the direction of the ball. I lost my balance, fell over. The ball was creeping past me. I had maybe ten or twenty hundredths of a second in which to reach the ball before I hit the ground again. It was 6-5 in the second set. Lendl had to win, otherwise he was dead. I was serving, but Lendl was leading 15-30. If I hadn't caught the

drop shot, it would have been 15-40 to Lendl, and he would have been away. In England I was like a wolf, in Paris I was soft. I couldn't even feel my feet on the carpets in that dump of a hotel. As I fell, I turned on my own axis. Hit the ball far away, I thought to myself. Diagonally, so he can't reach it. If I'd just played it over lamely, half-heartedly, Lendl would have got it. I over-stretched myself – and even if everything tore! – I couldn't let him reach it. I was on the ground, of course, although my line of sight was clear. He mustn't get it. And he didn't. That was when Lendl lost.'

On paper, the Final took 2 hours and 20 minutes. In reality, it lasted over 20 hours. The 'match fever' had begun the evening before; already, Boris's nervous system was burning up energy, reached its first climax when he woke, rising minute by minute until the Final on Sunday at 2 p.m. By the time the winning ball was played, his energy expenditure had drained about four litres of fluid out of him.

But the will to win had begun in Paris, with his revolt. Boris had put himself under pressure: 'I'll show those two ...' In spite of his youth, Boris is an experienced athlete. Pressure from outside drags him down. Pressure from inside gives him energy.

Wimbledon II was harder than Wimbledon I. In the first tournament, after all, it was all like a dream. If it went well – a miracle! If he lost, that was only normal. But now, the second time round? Of course, the spectators came and said, 'Man, where's the itch from last year? Just when we'd given him up, laid him to rest, earth on the grave, flowers, everything neat and tidy – and then, madness, the resurrection ...' That tickled everyone watching on TV. That's how he became a hero.

But now the hero was living a normal life, doing perfectly normal things. I told Boris he didn't have to play extraordinary tennis to win: 'Just play normally. Don't go over the top, don't crack up. Just play your usual game.' That made the second Wimbledon Final boring for a lot of people.

But it was at an incredible level. It was extraordinary tennis, his best game.

The Final in figures:
Wimbledon, 6 July 1986.
Boris Becker–Ivan Lendl 6-4, 6-3, 7-5.

	Becker	Lendl
First service in court	53%	53%
Baseline faults	7	9
Net faults	8	9
Double faults	7	6
Break points	9	6
Breaks	5	2
Direct points		
Aces	14	6
Service	23	21
Forehand	0	0
Backhand	1	2
Passing shots (forehand)	3	4
Passing shots (backhand)	2	6
Volleys	14	14
Smashes	4	3
Returns	8	8
Lobs	0	0
Drops	0	0
Total points		
Own score	69	64
Opponent's faults	24	22
Total	93	86

Wimbledon '86. They went on court as opponents, and came off as opponents. Boris has beaten the number one; but Lendl stays number one. The chase goes on

THERE'S ALWAYS
A STING IN THE TAIL

In the more than 5000 letters that Boris gets each month – many from people of his own age – there occur the words, 'If you write back, tell me what you're really like.'

You can see what he's like when he's playing, even though he's very retiring at present. He can make himself so incredibly happy that he does his 'shuffle'. Umpires have already warned him that this is unsportsmanlike; but he's just happy in himself, not malicious. Then he can sink to self-castigation in the same game.

What is Boris like? He doesn't feel things via his head – not even off court. When he lost in Mexico with the German Davis Cup team, in spite of winning both his singles matches, and with everyone else looking miserable, he said, 'Don't look like that – we have everything, we're all right.'

We had gone for a bit of a walk around Mexico City that evening, just a few streets round our hotel and had seen the begging children living in cardboard boxes on the street. 'Can't we put on an exhibition match for them? Ion must organize it.' We held an exhibition match for the children of Mexico.

UNICEF exhibition match in Washington: Boris and Vilas. In the middle, Dennis, mentally handicapped. Two thoughtful professionals, one happy Dennis

In Washington, he and Vilas played for the Handicapped Olympics, to be held in the USA in 1987. The organizers had chosen their opponents in the doubles match. Boris's partner – Dennis he was called – was a mentally retarded boy. Vilas's partner was physically handicapped.

Boris: 'I can't do it. It's macabre. I'm healthy and the boy is sick.'

But then they played after all. If Europeans understand America at all, it's only afterwards. Ion went out. When something gets to Ion, he disappears.

At first, Boris didn't know how he should play. Vilas was playing very carefully. Boris chased after Vilas's 'feather balls', threw himself at them. The mentally retarded boy began to laugh, clapped his hands. Suddenly, both professionals realized the way they should play. Both their partners should have fun.

In the hall, there were the big names in Washington, Foreign Secretary Schultz as protector, more than 20 ambassadors. I don't think they had tears in their eyes just for the cameras...

What's Boris like when we're alone?

When we're on our own, we work. He is noisy. He doesn't follow orders blindly. 'Convince me, then I'll do it.' He yells out whatever he feels. Our training is not a matter of learning strokes, but of repeating them over and over again for just the slightest improvement. A little improvement every day, that's the aim.

If I'm quiet for two minutes, he yells out,

'What's the matter? Aren't I doing anything wrong? What's the matter with my forehand? My backhand?' But never have we discussed the things we have to do each day: get up, eat breakfast, drive to the training session, train, lunch, rest, back to training again, dinner, in bed around 11, eleven hours' sleep.

That is something quite remarkable. I tell myself it's his lack of homesickness. Even as a kid, Boris was never homesick. I often had to remind him, 'Why don't you give them a ring?' He never rang home after losing, and still doesn't. If he rings up, it's because he's won. I think the tennis court is his den. All the tennis courts in the world look the same, which is why he never feels in a strange place or not at home.

To take the monotony out of training sessions, we change the exercises to avoid mindless routine.

Sometimes he complains I never praise him during training sessions. 'Tell me I'm good, I need it. A donkey couldn't keep up your training without some praise.'

I can't tell him he's good while he's training. Perhaps I'm wrong. There have been fierce arguments between Boris and me. 'You tell everyone how good they are, all the other players, except me,' he complained. 'You joke with everyone else during training sessions, but not with me.'

I'm afraid of too much praise. Praise can lose its effect as much as cursing. I praise him during games.

The workload in training sessions between tournaments is 20 per cent harder than during a match. Of course it's hard. My view is that there should be no pain, no weakness, no let-down in competitive matches that Boris has not already suffered and overcome in training. And there must be no praise. That's what it takes.

I won't mince words: we're out to get Lendl. Boris wants to be number one. He's set his mind on it. He says, 'Borg was a good number one, McEnroe was a good number one, Lendl is a bad number one.'

For me, too, Lendl is a bad number one. His game is methodical, he plays like a wound-up clock, very clever, but boring. But Lendl is the best athlete.

After Borg beat Lendl on the Supreme court in Chicago, Lendl's favourite ground, where he can use his speed, Lendl increased his training sessions by a third. I found that out later. Lendl lives in Greenwich, Connecticut, on a huge estate with jogging paths, gymnasium and his own tennis court. His estate is surrounded by high hedges, as if hiding a great secret. Legs, stamina, lungs, spring, speed – those are Lendl's tools. Lendl is the best craftsman out of the Top Ten. He would also be the best at throwing the javelin or the triple jump. We like Lendl as a person, but we don't like him on the throne of tennis.

For all our training in the mountains of Switzerland (interval running, sidesteps), there is one thing we have never been able to improve to any extent: Boris's basic speed. Out of the Top Ten, Boris is number nine for speed. He was born that way; it's something we have to put up with. For the first few metres, Ivan Lendl can keep up with top world-class sprinters. Wilander is perhaps not as fast as that, but compared with Boris he's like an arrow. If Boris hadn't been given two other weapons in compensation for his weary legs, two natural gifts, he would have no chance against Lendl. The first weapon is his

A service is too fast for the human eye to see. For this picture, Boris served in a darkened room. Using the stroboscopic effect (a special flash technique), his service is shown in six phases

Overleaf: *Using the same technique: a topspin backhand in full flow*

eyes, which struck me the first time I saw him. The second is his double-jointedness: Boris can bend his hand back to his lower arm, and touch his elbow with his index finger. Sometimes he shows this to journalists. I won't let him do it with his right hand: he might strain a tendon. He can do it with his left hand, although he's right-handed.

Now we are getting close to the heart of Boris. With his natural gift of being able to rotate his wrist through an incredible angle, he is in a position to whip up his forehand. There are pictures in this book showing his forehand in its most important phases. Together with his service, it is his main weapon. Using his wrist begins with his unusual grip – even this is a secret. Boris prefers an extreme eastern grip, very closed. The palm of his hand is along the side of the grip. This gives him the freedom his wrist requires. Now he is drawing back: his swing is much higher than any other player's. During a match, I am always signalling: Loosen your wrist, loosen your wrist....

Loosening the wrist gives the racket optimum acceleration – and at the moment when the racket hits the ball the wrist closes automatically, giving the ball an extra impetus – the 'crack' or the final twist. That's his whip, and, as with all whips, the sting is in the tail – from the wrist. It's a concealed stroke, since this automatic closing of the wrist happens at the last moment. The other player doesn't know where the ball's going until it's on its way. He can neither see nor anticipate it.

Serving uses up an enormous amount of energy. It's what breaks most players. By the fifth set, it's getting weaker and weaker. Boris holds his service when he's in form

What is Boris like? He is a child of fortune because he's never had a tennis lesson or a classical tennis teacher to impose a textbook technique on him. Then, as now, the fixed or solid wrist is taught. Boris plays the opposite way. I think the greatest mistake of tennis instructors is that they think they have to impose their idea of movement on their students. The correct way is the reverse: what special characteristics can the student provide? You can't work against Nature. We train on the forehand every day. All Boris's shots come from the heart.

Who is going to ask what's going on if he puts one foot in front of the other? You move. That's how simple it is. That's how simple the forehand is.

In the evenings, after training sessions, we go and eat. Usually we meet around 7.30 or 8.30 in the hotel foyer. By now, we know all the inside tips on city restaurants, but we also have our own favourites. This is where life after tennis begins.

These two or three hours are paradise for Boris. He looks forward to them all day. Paradise begins when he changes his clothes. Jeans, black shirt, jacket – all dark. Another skin. These three hours are all he has. I leave it up to him to decide who will be eating with us, where we'll go. This is his time to unwind. In New York, he likes going to Noah's Restaurant in Soho, run by three French friends of Noah's. Sometimes he goes off on his own. But only in New York, however crazy that sounds. New Yorkers are stars themselves, or at least they seem that way to me. 'Oh, hi!' they say, and go on their way.

For Boris, every nightspot is open, even if it is 'members only', or for the top ten thousand, or just full. During Wimbledon, we were staying at the Londonderry. Around the corner, there was the famous Hard Rock Café. 'Let's go there,' suggested Boris. There was a huge queue outside. First I thought people were queuing for theatre tickets; but no, like us, they wanted to get in. 'Boris, we haven't got a chance,' I said.

Boris kept going and took his place at the end of the queue. The people in the queue said, 'Please, Boris, come on, move up.' No one grumbled. They pushed us to the head of the queue. 'Come on, Boris.' And the policeman outside said, 'Please, Boris, come in.'

The owner appeared and arranged a table. On the walls, there were photos of all the rock stars, and there they were in person, sitting in front of us, next to us. It really is one of the world's most famous rock clubs. My ears hurt for hours afterwards, and the food was awful. A bit of meat and chips … a heap of food on a plate. The music was loud, but the queue outside got longer and longer, the crush inside was getting worse and worse. Were there two hundred or three hundred people there eating as well as us? The noise! I looked at Boris. I could see he wasn't thinking of tennis.

In April, six months before Wimbledon II, we were at a rock concert with Simple Minds, at Fort Worth, near Dallas. Noah, Edberg and Jarryd were there as well. Although Noah had pulled a fast one on Boris in Rome two years before (he pretended to be hurt and then swept Boris off the court the next day), they like each other a lot. As far as Boris is concerned, Noah is a character. Annacone isn't. Edberg is, Jarryd isn't. Connors is, Lendl isn't.

Under his denim jacket, Noah was wearing a red-flowered silk shirt. He had plaited his hair in little pigtails. Noah is the player who inspires Boris. Noah is one of the top ten players in the world, even though he smokes, has a wife, a child and a restaurant in New York. For Boris, Noah is a phenomenon because he manages to stay at the top of the world and live as well. Boris ruffled Noah's hair; Noah lets him do that.

I like it when they train together. In training with Noah, Boris manages shots which wouldn't be out of place in a circus. And suddenly, he runs easily. Against players like Annacone or Wilkison, his legs seem heavy and stumpy. Against Noah, they are elegant, incredibly agile. Noah spurs him on to play like Noah himself: easily and elegantly.

This ease has to do with his masochism. Let me explain. Boris gets a kick out of beating Wilander from the baseline with high topspins. Baseline play is Wilander's weapon. Boris tries to beat him at his own game. He also tries to beat

Noah with artistic tennis. Pure Utopia. Stefan Edberg, for instance, is a born serve-and-volley player. Boris just plays Stefan at his own game. Lendl's greatest weapon is his forehand. Boris doesn't play to his weaker backhand, but lets himself in for a forehand duel because he wants to show Lendl that his forehand is better.

That isn't normal. All players try to cut out their opponents' strengths, not to let them use these strengths in the game. Boris challenges their strengths. He could just play to Lendl's weak left-hand side. But he doesn't. He plays to his forehand. Forehand in Wimbledon, backhand in Chicago. It's masochism: he deliberately makes things hard for himself.

He beat Connors aggressively. In Chicago, he scarcely used his own weapons against Connors: returns, service, the forehand smash. He battled Connors down. He picked up points you'd usually give up as lost. He threw himself around, ran himself into the ground and roared at himself. The match went on for nearly three hours.

Once, Connors lobbed the ball up to him; Boris lobbed it back. Boris couldn't get round the ball any further, so he hit it between his legs. Connors played a drop shot; Boris reached it. They tormented each other. The battle went on for minutes. The crowd were going wild.

Once, when they were changing ends, Boris told Connors, 'You're too old to play like that.' Connors hissed back, 'Don't worry about how old I am.' An incredible fight. Boris wanted to be a better Connors than Connors.

I don't know where he gets it from. That's just the way it is: in-born. I can remember a match in Lippstadt against Gehring; Boris was not yet fifteen. Gehring is a very sensitive player who can play very good drop shots and all the things for which you need a special feel. Even then, Boris could have wiped Gehring off the court with his shots. I thought I was seeing things: Boris was playing like Gehring! Drops where he could have smashed; exquisite lobs where a rock-hard volley would have been a dead certain point. He wanted to show Gehring with each ball that he had as much feeling as he did. He let himself in for a very complicated match, which Boris won in the final result – but what an effort!

In the German Embassy car park, Washington. The big names in Washington are still inside: Ethel Kennedy, General Haig, Foreign Secretary Schultz. Boris has slipped out, and waits for the chauffeur

Of course, we have discussed his masochism. When we do, he says the same thing now as he did then. 'I don't think about it ... At first, I just play my own game. But if the other player plays three smashes at me, I play three back. It's the other player who starts it. If he uses a drop shot, I use one back. If he smashes a long forehand at me, I smash a long forehand back. If someone thinks they have a better stroke than me, I use it back at them, and keep on using it until they soften up.'

There is a tactic that says that in world-class tennis, first you have to destroy the other player's strengths, then his weaknesses. But for that, you have to be a very strong player. I'm all for this tactic, since he has it in him.

When I'm out driving with Boris – with him at the wheel – I get frightened. Like any boy of his age, he likes driving fast in Monaco, along the

coast and mountain roads to Nice, or over to Italy – he knows every bend in the road.

Well, maybe at nearly fifty I'm too fearful, because he drives well, with concentration. Nevertheless, we're always in trouble. Once, overtaking coming up to a bend, he claimed he could see round it; and anyway, he just *guessed* there was nothing coming....

He was using the American expression 'guess' – a favourite expression amongst tennis players. When it comes to driving, however, I'd rather he just wiped this expression from his mind. In tennis, on the other hand, guessing is his major weapon. His opponent plays a drop shot. Boris is already moving before the ball is over the net. He 'foresees the ball'. Other players only see it very late, but manage it because they're very fast. Lendl can reach it.

This second sight or feeling is important when it is the other player serving. Lendl, whose service is one of the best in the world, only managed six aces against Boris in the Final at Wimbledon. Boris was always already in position to return Lendl's service. Boris managed 14 aces against Lendl. Boris is the better 'guesser'.

Am I writing too much about Lendl?

At present, there is only him. The duel continues....

At the American Open Championships in Flushing Meadow in 1986, Lendl fired the first shot in the war of words. On television, he said, 'It doesn't matter if it's Becker or my grandmother in the tournament. The main thing is for me to play well and win.' In a newspaper interview, he said Boris was arrogant.

The other player serves. Boris waits for the ball. Every player has his or her own starting position, where they feel good. Boris's stance can't be found in any textbook: legs apart, rocking to and fro, he waits for the ball

And elsewhere: 'Tiriac will destroy him because Boris was a nice guy before Tiriac came along.'

Boris challenged Lendl in the changing-rooms: 'What was that you said about me?'

Lendl was cool. 'I was misquoted.'

The duel of the next two years is Lendl v. Boris. The deciding factor will either be Lendl's speed on his feet or Boris's 'guessing'.

Guessing is a war of nerves and eyes when it is the opponent to serve.

This is how the battles of the future will go: Lendl will have to win his services because he must assume that Boris, with his stronger service, will win his.

Who will get the chance to make the break – the better runner or the better guesser? In Chicago, for instance, Lendl only managed two aces. Every other time he served, Boris got to the ball.

How does this guessing work?

How can I help him here as trainer? Two years ago, I would shout, 'Look at the racket head, look at the grip, look at the feet. Remember what the service was like in different situations. How did you serve when it was your advantage? At deuce? When leading 30-0?' In the class they're both playing in, these are understood, like the alphabet or the times tables. Lendl hits the ball as secretively as Boris. Each look deceives. It's a poker game.

Lendl will look to the right-hand corner of the service box, bouncing the ball at the same time. He bounces the ball several times. Will he hit it to the right-hand corner? On the second bounce, he looks towards the left-hand corner. Now, on the third bounce, again to the left. You can't tell anything from his stance or his grip. Any player in this class can change his stance in a hundredth of a second. Correction: the first seven can.

What's going on in Boris's mind? He must return the shot.

'I'm waiting,' says Boris.

'Are you nervous?' I ask.

'No.'

'Do you feel afraid?'

'No.'

But then he strikes. He can earn his points with a single shot.

'I'm looking. While I'm looking, I decide on a corner, left or right. I have to do that with Lendl, otherwise I haven't a chance. When he hits the ball, I have to be in a corner. Right or not. His service comes as fast as mine – about 150 miles an hour. Most of the time, I watch. I just watch him. When he's getting ready to serve, when he bounces the ball for the first time, I can see through his eyes. At some point, I choose a corner and wait. I move left, watch him and wait. He keeps on bouncing the ball. I stay over on the left, leaving the right-hand corner open to him. Just before he makes up his mind, I 'castle' and change sides. I don't use sidesteps, I swing from side to side with the upper half of my body.

'Maybe he's made his mind up long ago. But I can influence it. Now, he serves – either I have him or I don't. The next shot he makes, I do the same. When the score reaches 30-all, I tell myself, "Win or lose". Then luck decides. But I don't know that myself at that moment. What's important is that I forget all the moves the other player has made. I must follow my own guidance if I'm to have any chance. Sometimes it's crystal-clear, it goes through you and you know. I'm sure Lendl sometimes also feels which way I'm going to serve. Normally, you never get to the ball unless you sense it in advance. My balls arrive as fast as his. He has to sense them.'

That's 'guessing'.

I can recall many games in my mind, going over the serves with the advantage of hindsight. I notice every movement the other player makes. Only rarely do I notice their service. My explanation is that they are playing in a trance,

Boris in trouble. Right at the edge of the court. A backhand volley. Boris's chances of reaching it aren't good. The other player is already at the net

The Davis Cup. For Boris, the greatest thing is playing for Germany. In the Davis Cup, he's not playing for himself but for Germany. The Davis Cup is a team competition: a contradiction in tennis because tennis is an individual sport. For that reason alone, the Davis Cup is something special. The pressure is different, incredible. 'I'm playing for my country, for everyone.' **Above:** *Warming-up training in Hamburg against the USA with Andreas Maurer (right), his doubles partner.* **Below:** *Maurer leaps into Boris's arms, as they beat Lendl and Smid in Frankfurt*

The pressure on Boris is enormous. By now, he has had to win both his own two singles matches – and usually the doubles match as well. In Frankfurt, things went OK; but not against the Swedes in Munich: Boris the one-man team lost 2-3. **Above:** Boris beats Mecir in Frankfurt 1985. **Left:** Boris also beats Wilander in the final in Munich. We trained in Sarnen (Switzerland) for ten days for the Davis Cup. His sparring partner was Slobodan 'Bobo' Zivojinovic. Bobo is our friend; he is one of the top 20, and Boris's real doubles partner

Left: *Boris as spectator. Westphal v. Edberg. Westphal loses. Afterwards, Boris said, 'Now I know what you're going through out there. You die out there.'*

Above: *Bungert, the captain, during a coaching session. Boris drinks, Bungert looks straight ahead*

Overleaf: *The winning Swedes. Boris, the loser, laughs with the winners. First he congratulates Mats Wilander. Boris won both his singles matches. Back in the changing-rooms, he was downcast: Germany had lost*

their nerves are ultra-sensitized. Lendl guesses as well. He sees that Boris is going to hit the ball one way or the other. I know Boris very well, but I can't guess how he is going to serve.

The return of service is the most terrifying thing in the way the Top Ten play tennis. After such a shot, people often ask me, 'Those shots – how can a mere human being even catch them, let alone return them?'

The Top Ten don't play with ordinary mortals. Sometimes Boris will play a few balls with his mother or sister. Once, he made an exception. At the UNICEF exhibition matches in Washington, US Foreign Secretary Schultz had invited Boris and Vilas to a doubles match at the White House. Next to the helicopter pad in front of the President's Oval Office is a beautiful hard court surrounded by bushes and hedges. The players were Schultz, Vilas, the son of Vice-President Bush and Boris. Ion was the umpire, I was the coach.

When the match was over, Schultz said to Boris, 'I've been playing tennis for forty years; give me a serve like you would serve against Lendl. I'd like to see what it's like, just for once.'

Boris hit two aces. Schultz didn't move.

'Thanks, Boris,' said Schultz, as he said good-bye. 'I didn't see your serves.'

A normal reaction would be flight, retreat in the face of a ball arriving at 150 m.p.h.

Boris goes after the ball, picks it up. He blocks it just in front of his body. Forehand, backhand – it makes no difference to him.

I call that kind of shot a 'return ace'; usually it's a clear point.

Does it take courage to go for such a ball? McEnroe had it once, Boris has it. I don't know any other players at the moment who can play such 'return aces'.

Is the ball in, or what? The ball is on the line; Boris looks at the line judge. He played a return. There are twelve line judges on court. In or out? When the decision is made, Boris's querying face will radiate joy or annoyance

PURE BORIS

Dallas, Saturday 12 April 1986. A terrible, beautiful day. Boris has just beaten Edberg in the semi-finals, in four dramatic sets with three tie-breaks, 7-6, 7-6, 4-6, 7-6. Yesterday, he beat Annacone 7-5, 7-5, 6-1. Tomorrow, Sunday, he is due to meet Anders Jarryd in the final of the unofficial WCT world championships. Out of 44 hours, he has spent 10 on court: pure Boris.

I've put the 44 hours at Dallas on tape because they show Boris and me at work.

We were staying at the Hyatt Regency Hotel, an ultra-modern box with a blue-green mirrored front. (You can see it in the titles of the *Dallas* series on TV.)

Saturday ... The semi-finals are set for 10.30 a.m. I haven't seen anything of the city except this hotel. The car service takes us the 400 yards to the Reunion Arena, to the tennis facilities. The car service takes us back to the hotel. A few streets away from the Hyatt is the place where John F. Kennedy was shot. I had to see the depository from whose window the assassin took his aim. At that time, I was living in Romania. I think that anyone who was alive at that time knows exactly what he or she was doing on that

The 'Boris shuffle'. He only does it on special occasions: the shots he nearly missed, but managed to win. Boris is the first player in the world to dance for joy on court

22nd of November. I was training the Romanian national youth team. Then came the terrible news....

Dust to dust ... We had arranged to meet for breakfast at 7.30.

I was ten minutes late because I'd been tensioning an eighth racket just to be on the safe side. It was a best-of-five match, three sets to win. Sometimes this sort of match can last for three or four hours. Better safe than sorry.

'Why are you late? What's the matter?'

I told him.

'OK, OK.'

He was on edge; every little thing upset him.

'These cards, all these cards,' he puffed.

In front of a plate of fruit, there was a stack of autograph cards for him to sign.

'Ion gave you those last night,' I said. 'You should have autographed them immediately ... not now, not before the match.' I put the cards in my training bag.

He was looking for an argument. 'Why do I have to sign all these thousands of cards?'

'The group which has a contract with you wants to give them to its business friends.'

'Why is it always me?' His eyes glared.

No match day is like any other; this one was terrible. On some match days, I have to build up his aggression. Aggression and a bit of fear – that's the balance needed. On the day of the match, he must be a fighter. 'I'll kill him, I'll beat him ...' An aggressive fighting – almost killer – instinct has to be there; but at the same time a

131

certain relaxation, enormous concentration, mixed with fear. Not fright, fear. There must be fear nagging at him so that he doesn't go into a match over-confident.

It's all very contradictory: aggression, relaxation, the ability to switch off with a cool, clear head, the feeling of fear. He has to be greedy, but not blind.

Before competition matches, I talk to him softly, quietly.

'Listen to me,' I say. 'Fight, win the match by fighting. The beginning is important: give him a shock right at the beginning, make the first break as fast as you can.'

When we're playing abroad, and I know that the match will be shown on TV in Germany, I tell him, 'They're broadcasting your match back home ... Get stuck in ...' Those are more or less the last words as he goes out on court. 'Get stuck in.' It really motivates him when he knows that his matches will be watched in Germany.

Now, over breakfast, I might as well have saved my breath. He is near to bursting. How are we going to bring him down? I ask myself. He is bursting with aggression. His eyes are slightly enlarged, they're piercing. He is in a state of great tension.

'Couldn't sleep,' he says. 'Did you hear the storm in the night?'

'Did it disturb you?'

'This time it did.'

Me: 'I open the curtains. Open the curtains if there's thunder, then you can work out where you are more easily.'

Boris: 'I can't sleep when there's thunder.'

He was sitting in front of me with his legs crossed, his shoulders hunched. At this class, tennis has little to do with the noble white sport. The Top Ten are no different from football players or boxers.

Training. Boris asks me for another ball. He already had 101 services behind him that day; this was number 102

Training. Forehand topspin: Boris's No. 2 weapon. This is what his opponents fear most (next to his service). He 'kills' the high balls from midfield with his whip-like movement and drags them down. You can't get to number one with a weak forehand

Forehand volley: Boris still had yet to master this shot when he won Wimbledon. It was his weak point. When he lost to Schapers in Australia, we practised forehand volleys six hours a day for two weeks. Before that, he was just 'stirring the soup'; now he's good

The backhand. Sixty per cent of our training time is devoted to backhand shots. Everyone expects Boris's backhand to be like his forehand; but, anatomically speaking, his chest is in the way, his swing is limited. Backhand takes precision timing, exact movements. There are specialists: Mats Wilander, for instance

Backhand volley. Boris does 20 press-ups a day for this shot. Most of the strength it requires is in the wrist: you only have your thumb for resistance (or the four fingers for the forehand). The results of power training: above his serving arm elbow, you can see his backhand volley muscles sticking out

137

'I'll go and get my things', he said.

'There's another three and a half hours to the match,' I said soothingly. 'No rush.'

As he stood up, his chair fell over backwards. Ion picked it up.

'There's tension in the air,' I said to Ion, after he had gone. 'We'll have to watch out.'

Our programme until the match was fixed. From 8.30 to 9.30, training, then massage, then an hour of mental preparation with all the stretching exercises.

We went on eating our breakfast. I assumed that Boris would come and pick us up when he had got his things. He didn't turn up. I waited and waited. Nothing happened. Suddenly, I heard him shouting, 'Coach, where are you? What's the matter? I've been waiting half an hour in the lobby for you!'

It wasn't true.

'No hurry,' I said. 'There's time enough.'

'Yes, but Edberg is bound to be training as well. I want to be alone on the court.'

We were alone. By that, I mean Edberg hadn't turned up yet. But of course, we're never alone. Before such a semi-final as this, the television people were getting their cameras ready, the stewards were there, the first spectators, officials and journalists.

The warming-up session should always be held on the court where the match itself is to take place. The player must see the surroundings once more, his eyes must get used to the light conditions. He must get the feel for the ball – foot contact is important. In Dallas, we were playing on a Supreme surface, a fast court. I always arranged the warming-up session the same way: first the basic strokes, then fly balls, smashes, and last the service. To finish with, he simulated shots that might occur during the match. Edberg always comes up very close, right to the net. For that reason, I decided to practise lobs with him.

We began with the basic strokes. Things started going wrong with the first ball I played to him. 'Hey, what are you playing to me? ... Drill, drill!' he yelled – I couldn't understand what he was saying.

Ion, who was collecting up the balls behind me

and throwing them to me, said, 'We'll have to bring him down. He's cracking up.'

'Drill, drill!' Boris was screaming. Now I knew what he meant. He wanted me to hit the balls into the corners, so he would run more, use his body energy up. He wanted me to run him into the ground.

He was on the point of exploding. I was a player myself. You can look for a thousand and one ways to get it out of your system. He does it deliberately. He controls it. When he woke up early that morning, he deliberately raised his adrenalin level. But now he couldn't control himself any longer. He was lashing out at anything around him.

'Drill!' he shouted at me.

'Drill! Drill!' I shouted back.

Considering that I'm forty-eight, I'm not a bad tennis player. But I'm not number six or seven in the world. I can't hurl the balls at him the way Edberg can.

'Drill!' he roared again. He wanted me to wear him down. But I'm not one of the Top Ten.

Then Edberg turned up. He stood at the side of the court. It was nearly 9.30. Edberg wanted to warm up. The fact that he was there, watching, unnerved Boris.

'That's it, I'm finished!' he shouted, took his things and rushed off without waiting for me.

'That's torn it,' I said to Ion.

It was the first time he'd left me behind on court. We have a rule that if we come on court together, we go off court together.

For the first time, he left alone.

I could have told him what I thought. Perhaps any other trainer would have done just that: 'You do that just once more and....'

I swallowed my feelings. Like a lightning conductor, I took a deep breath, and tried to calm down a bit. Then I followed him to our box. If I'd confronted him there, things would have been bad. Boris is extreme. He is the way he plays. He suffers, he dances. He jumps out of the window.

In the box, it was as if nothing had happened. Not a word about what had happened. We scrubbed the programme.

If I wasn't convinced that Boris is an exceptional athlete, I wouldn't be able to coach him. A player like Boris comes along perhaps once in twenty years.

I sat down quietly beside him. 'Listen to me,' I said. 'Play a lot of lobs today. Every other passing shot from you has to be a lob because Edberg will have the net covered. He comes up close to the net and cuts off all the corners. Lobs are all you've got left. Listen to me.'

I was deliberately making my words very measured. I hoped it would get through to Boris.

'It doesn't matter if you make a mistake now and then. You've got to show Edberg you'll be playing lobs, then he won't dare get so close to the net.'

Eye to eye, by a kind of thought transmission, I tried to instill the tactics in him.

A player lives on his memories. The nearer the match comes, the more he suppresses unpleasant memories, avoids negative thoughts. He thinks: 'I beat Edberg the last two times [Las Vegas, Davis Cup in Munich], I'm going to beat him this time.' His memory forgets that once all he could do was lose to Edberg.

It's like whistling in the dark. You're walking alone through the woods at night – and you whistle. You're trying to make believe you couldn't care less, and – if you really convince yourself – you really *couldn't* care less. It's my job to worm my way into these thought processes and somehow admit the possibility of defeat. Not to intimidate Boris, but to keep him alert.

'Listen,' I said. 'In the junior matches, Edberg always beat you. You know what he can do. He plays the best backhand passing shot in the world, the second-best forehand cross-court passing shot, and he's got the best twist service in the world. And he always comes straight to the net. Your chance is the lob. Use it again and again.'

With the twist serve, as anyone in tennis knows, the ball goes very high, and is very difficult to return. It's a shot that really amazes me.

In the preparatory phase, no one was with us in the cabin, not even Ion Tiriac. You're very helpless in the hour before a match. Your nerves are laid bare. We'd forgotten about the warming-up incident. In this phase nothing could be allowed to come between us. I mustn't have any problems. Nor must Boris.

I don't know what it would be like if Boris had a problem with a girl, a very personal problem. I have a daughter of twenty-three. There are some things she can talk about, others she can't, not even with my wife. These deep, intimate matters dominate and besiege all other feelings, the will to succeed, the ego. Since as a father I had an idea how shy eighteen-year-olds can be, and because I know Boris, because I knew how far he could let himself go and how deeply he felt, I was a bit afraid.

Before a match, there must be calm, no alien thoughts must intrude. The only thoughts must be about the match. If I say here that there in the changing-rooms I felt the same itch as Boris, that might sound like an exaggeration. But it's the truth. The itch is incredible. We kept ourselves warm. By the way he moved, I could tell that the urge to beat Edberg burnt in him like a madness. The shameful defeat against Wilkison in Atlanta, when he got knocked out in the first round, was two weeks ago. Now he wanted to show them all. His flipping out over breakfast, his aggressiveness ... Sometimes I wonder if Ion and I make too many demands of him. But were we still in control?

Even without winning at Wimbledon, Boris would still be among the Top Ten in the world; but his whole development would have been more 'normal', more comprehensible to himself and us. Boris, Ion and I were all hiding behind flak-jackets, because we were under fire from all sides. When would he be number one? There's no such thing as peaceful development. There wasn't just the German public, there were the Americans, the Canadians, the British ... Boris must be number one! Boris is everyone's flirtation with winning. The red-blond eighteen-year-old has become a general, international hero. And I, his coach, and Ion, his manager, have been dragged along with him. Further and further....

I had to stop Boris eating grapes: their sugar content didn't fit into his eating programme. But Boris loved grapes. Isn't that absurd, isn't it crazy? A healthy eighteen-year-old boy, not

allowed to eat grapes? I didn't begrudge him his rude, aggressive behaviour earlier that day because it's we who keep him in this extreme world of feeling on account of his exceptional talent.

In front of the cabins in Dallas there is a long corridor. Now we did short sprints, then skipping and jumping like boxers preparing for a fight. Now the stretch exercises, right, then left. I repressed my pangs of conscience about driving him so hard because he wouldn't have it any other way. He wouldn't be happy any other way.

Now he was running on the spot, taking the small, vital boxer's steps. It is these little steps that decide the match: flexible, aware. Long strides may win the 5000-metre races, but they don't win tennis matches. We worked for an hour. The muscles, the sinews, the joints all had to be softened and warmed up, he had to be sweating when he went on to court.

We still had half an hour. From the eight rackets, he chose the one he would play with; although he didn't look consciously, he just picked one out instinctively. All eight rackets were the same, new, all had the same catgut stringing. The stringing depends on the ball and the court. The harder the ball, the harder the stringing. The harder and faster the ball flies through the air, the harder the strings must be. Likewise, the harder the court, the harder the strings. Before matches on slow courts in Europe such as on sand or rain-heavy ground, we set the strings softer. The moisture also makes the ball heavier, another reason for softer stringing. Now, on a hard surface and with fast balls, we set the lengthways strings at 31 kilos and the cross strings at 29 kilos.

Boris in Texas. He didn't have time to go riding in Dallas or visit the South Fork ranch: out of 44 hours there, he spent 10 on court. Eleven long sets, four tie-breaks. And that's not counting training sessions

Left: *Boris's face is stony during a backhand slice. He is on the attack. His eyes are fixed on the oncoming ball: he wants to hit it as far in front of his body as possible*

Above: *Preparing for a smash*

Now Boris was hitting imaginary balls. Like a slalom skier going through the gates in his mind, he was imagining the game. It was fantastic: he was programming himself. Boris was in his cabin, but in his thoughts he was already out on the court. He could see Edberg on the other side of the net. Over the way, in his cabin, Edberg was playing the same shadow tennis.

When the Top Ten play tennis, they don't just go out there and start playing, only starting to think in certain situations whether to go forward or stay back. The players know one another, know each other's reactions and reflexes off pat. Each player lives on his memories. As far as these are concerned, they have brains like computers or data records.

'With that ball, I did so-and-so … When I stood there, he played such-and-such….'

Now I was as soaked through with sweat as Boris was. I share his life with him. If it didn't affect me, if my pulse wasn't as fast as his, it would irritate him. In exhibition matches, when I'm more relaxed, he says, 'Hey, I've got a match to play, how come you're so calm?'

He feels every emotion.

My hands were cold, I felt incredibly restless. If I say that my lower jaw was shaking a bit, that's no exaggeration. I was afraid of Edberg; but fright is the wrong word, it was more a kind of cold-blooded funk.

That's the coach's problem: he isn't down there on court, he's up in the stands. Down there is where it all happens. OK, sometimes I can kick a pillar or hammer a desk with my fist. I actually hurt myself when Boris makes a mistake. I leap in the air when he plays a good shot. I experience the game the way he does. And yet: he's the one playing, not me … I daren't show him the way I feel inside. I mustn't let him see that my hands are cold or that I'm boiling over inside. Now the trick is to instill calm in him. Before the match and during it.

For a long time now, there has been an umpire at each tournament whose only job is to watch my hands and face, to see if I'm secretly coaching Boris during the match. Of course I'm coaching. I play every ball with him. Now there can be no indifference. During the match, Boris will look up at me, even when things are going well. He looks up for confirmation. 'Hey, coach, I played that one well, didn't I?' I nod. That's normal. It was a good shot, and he's pleased. All he needed was confirmation. Nothing more. I'm as pleased as he is. I nod, he plays on. That's all it is.

In La Quinta, I clapped after a good shot, we laughed at each other. 'Bravo, well done!' It was a shot we had practised in training. He got a warning for illegal coaching, and had a point taken off him.

During the match with Edberg, I went quite mad. 'Play lobs!' I yelled at him. 'You've got to play lobs.' At 5-all, with Edberg to serve, Boris was leading 30-0, he had a chance to make it 40-0, and the set was virtually won. Edberg served – a twist – and rushed forward. But then, Boris got the lob wrong. He played it very half-heartedly, as if clammed up. I got incredibly worked up. I signalled to him, 'Play lobs. Nothing else.' But inside, that wasn't what he wanted to do.

There are boys who always do the opposite of what their father tells them. I think this was rebellion on Boris's part, and I really got worked up. Inside himself, he didn't want to play a lob. He played it half across Edberg, despondently – and of course Edberg caught it, smashed it back to make the score 30-15. The smash gave Edberg courage, and he won his service game.

When the players sat down, Boris flipped. He raged up at me, 'Wrong coaching! I have to do everything myself. No one gives me any help. Wrong coaching, wrong coaching.'

There were 17,000 spectators in the stadium; the game was being broadcast on both German and American television. Millions were watching it on TV. For the first time, Boris insulted me. 'Nuts!' he cried.

Ion was sitting next to me. 'Tell me, have I done something wrong?' I asked.

'He's your boy,' Ion said coldly. 'You should have brought him up better.'

'Time,' the umpire called. My boy went out on the court.

Of the three of us, people think Ion is hard and I am soft. Am I soft to just sit there and take insults? Would the tough thing be to stand up and leave? That would be the wrong kind of hardness.

I saw it out, stayed sitting down, kept on coaching him. It came to a tie-break.

A minute later, the situation called for a lob again. 'Lob,' I signalled. The link between us had not snapped. I yelled at him. No one could hear me 'yelling'. I lifted my right hand, forced

---

Tiriac and I. Between us: Tiriac's office: his satellite telephone. Eighty per cent of his business is done by phone. Purchase price: 3000 dollars. He takes it with him everywhere, even to matches

146

Boris floored. He collapses after throwing himself at the ball like a goalkeeper. He gets back up, wondering. While changing ends, his face shows his despair. In his mind, he wonders, 'What did I do wrong? How can I turn the match round?'

him to play a lob. It was a transfer of will. I *wanted* that lob.

He played it. It was an incredible lob.

He won the tie-break, and the set.

'Your set,' Boris laughed up at me. He sat down and got up again. 'You won that one, coach.'

Edberg and Boris played for over three and a half hours. There were scenes of incredible drama. In the fourth set, Boris played a drop shot. Edberg ran towards the net, didn't get it, but he had such momentum that he couldn't stop himself and leapt over the net towards Boris.

Boris put his arm round Edberg's shoulder. You could see they were both finished. Standing ovations. The court rocked.

Two world-class players fighting bitterly, fighting for each point – and then this scene. It got to everyone. Everyone could feel how lonely the players were down there.

'Boris, I'm so slow,' Edberg said to him (so Boris told me later). 'You'll get the next one,' Boris comforted him.

Edberg went back to his side of the court, and Boris beat him 7-6, 7-6, 4-6, 7-6.

Normally, after a match is over, I wait for Boris at the Centre Court exit. Usually he has to say a few words for the cameras; that usually takes a few minutes. I stood there by the exit and held out my hand to him when he came out with his bags. 'Well played, Boris, thanks, bravo.' We left together; by this time, that had become a ritual.

But now, for the first time, I wasn't waiting for him. He went alone to his cabin, I went to mine. On the way over, some journalists wanted to talk to me about Boris's outbursts. I played it down: 'Oh, the things you say you've seen or heard....'

Boris's box was on the right, mine on the left. When I came in, he was sitting in my box. 'I'm sorry. I'm sorry for what I did,' he said. 'You're the only one who understands me.'

Was it soft of me to accept his apology? But can you ask more of a man than for him to say he's sorry? Later, in three or four days' time, once the tournament was over, I'd have another talk with him about it.

We had 30 minutes for him to calm down. His body was still playing, the muscles twitching. As the winner, he didn't have to be at the press conference first: it's the loser who has to face the reporters first. That's an awful thing. You have to analyse your game, explain why you lost. You mustn't show your feelings, mustn't let it show how furious and sad you are inside, that what you'd really like to do is howl with rage, incomprehension and despair. When you're worked up after a match, it's hard to face the press. Boris often says, 'The journalists try and make me tell them lies. I don't want to lie to them. But if I told them how I really felt they'd tear me to shreds.'

Players respect the loser's pain. They treat losers with care. Journalists are after a story, they burrow around in the wounds. I was impressed by the way Wilander behaved towards Boris in Australia after the Schapers defeat. Boris was sitting in the changing rooms, his head in his hands. Wilander, who had just finished his doubles match, came in. News of the sensational defeat had of course got around amongst the players long ago. Wilander was quiet, said nothing, had a shower, changed his clothes, avoided making any noise, and went back out on tiptoe. Once I saw Noah crying after being beaten. No one looked at him. Everyone looked away. Not a word was ever said about it, then or afterwards.

A winner doesn't want to go to bed, can't turn off: he wants to prolong the victory, savour it. He just doesn't want the feeling to end. As coach, you never stop being a coach. How long should Boris go on being happy for? How long should he mourn? You mustn't mourn too long after a

defeat, nor celebrate too much after winning. And if you make each defeat a funeral, the only one to die in the end will be you. In Atlanta, after two big celebrations in Chicago – winning against Connors and Lendl – he lost to Wilkison. Even before he'd won, I knew he'd have to face Wilkison in Atlanta. 'You'll be playing Rambo,' I warned him. 'Watch out, he'll tear you to bits on court.' The professionals call Wilkison 'Rambo' because of the aggressive way he plays, after the muscle-bound film hero who wins the Vietnam war belatedly for the United States on screen.

'So what?' said Boris. 'I'm an animal too.' After the two celebrations, there was no more talk of Boris the animal. 'I'll beat him elegantly.'

This time, there was no time for celebrating after beating Edberg. The Final had been set for the morning. At 11 p.m., Boris went to bed. After the Final, he had to be first at the press conference. He lost to Jarryd 7-6, 1-6, 1-6, 4-6. He told the reporters that he'd gone into the game with an injury: because of muscle fibrosis in his right thigh, he'd virtually only been able to play with one leg.

I didn't accept his excuse. I was mad at him. OK, something had been wrong with his thigh the week before, but he'd been fit to play. He'd beaten Edberg the day before with the same thigh, and Annacone before that. Boris is always hypochondriac before matches. I didn't take him seriously. 'Oh, I can't run, I'm dying, my legs . . .' Often, he invokes the pain himself, because for him, desperation is adrenalin.

During the press conference, I stood by the door. I said nothing. We went back to the box together. I let his body calm down. It would have been unfair to make him talk just then.

Ion knocked at the door. 'What's up? Are we flying to Japan or aren't we? If we are, then hurry up.'

We had exhibition tournaments in Tokyo and Hong Kong two days later. The plane left in three hours: Dallas–New York–Tokyo.

'I've hurt myself,' said Boris.

There's an awful lot of money involved in these exhibition matches.

'What do you mean, injured?' Ion asked.

Forest Hills – the only tournament in the world played on green sand. At first I thought the Americans had coloured the sand green; but it really is green, it comes from Canada. Boris allows himself to use the forehand

149

'I can't do it,' said Boris.

Ion and I are often at loggerheads over these exhibition matches. I don't want Boris chasing round the world. I want to have long recovery periods between major competitive tournaments. But money rules the world. I know that too.

'I've hurt myself,' said Boris. 'No.'

He was giving up a lot of money with that answer.

Ion choked on Boris's 'No', but said nothing. Ion has a satellite telephone: it weighs about four kilos, he always carries it around with him, wherever he is in the world: in the plane, in the car, by the swimming pool, he can call anyone, and anyone can call him. He cancelled the exhibition matches. The Japanese demanded a medical certificate. Their 'commercials', their advertising, had been built around Boris. They started talking about contract penalties ... Ion made one call after another. He takes this side of our life off our hands.

The other side, between Boris and me, still had to be sorted out. It was the first time Boris had given an injury as a reason for a defeat. It had been the other way round for as long as I'd known him: injuries built him up, he overcame them, forgot them in the match. I had to know what had happened to him in that match.

Chaos! The reporters had more questions, Ion had fixed other flights – Dallas, New York, Paris, Nice. The flight left in an hour.

Boris said, 'I'm not going. I don't want to see another aeroplane today. I'll fly tomorrow.'

Ion: 'Do what you like, I'm going.'

Two hours later, I called Boris in his room. 'Let's go and have a salad.'

We met in the Hyatt Regency coffee shop.

'Has someone died?' he asked me, when he saw my face.

'Well, whoever it was, it wasn't you on court.'

'What?'

'I don't think you gave everything.'

I wanted to sort out the matter of insults. I can only work with the Boris I know. I think people like Boris because he plays without any tricks or any internal excuses. Either he 'dies' on court or he lives.

By the look on my face, Boris could see it was serious. In the coffee shop, he pulled his socks off and showed me the blood blisters on the soles of his feet as he held his thigh.

'I couldn't jump any more when I was serving. All I could do were throw-ins.'

There were people, I said, who had toothache they could hardly stand and yet, once they were sitting in the dentist's chair, all at once the pain was gone. 'The body always does what the mind tells it to. If you want to, you can feel no pain.'

He stood up and hobbled off.

Later, I apologized to him for those words. He *had* hurt himself. In Monte Carlo, specialists recognized the muscle fibrosis. As a boy, Boris had fallen on a pane of glass. The fibrosis in his right thigh stemmed from that old wound....

There were the 44 hours at Dallas. Of those 44 hours, Boris spent 10 on court. He'd beaten Annacone on Friday, Edberg on Saturday morning, lost to Jarryd on Sunday morning. Eleven long sets, with four tie-breaks.

All we did was work; we didn't see anything of the city. Boris had bought himself some cowboy boots, that was all. At 11 a.m. on Monday we flew out. We'd been travelling without a break for ten weeks: California, Mexico, Brussels, Chicago, Atlanta, Washington, Dallas. If he hadn't hurt himself, he would have been playing in Hong Kong that day.

Boris was wearing his travelling clothes: the black 'disguise' hat my wife had given him, black sunglasses, jeans, black shirt, dark jacket, Walkman. If looks could have killed, Boris would have been full of holes. You can't avoid people's looks all the time, but they're easier to take behind black sunglasses. We felt like workers coming off a shift. If anyone asked me what image we'd seen most often in the last ten weeks – apart from the outlines of the tennis court – I'd have to say the clouds below us ... and people next to us and in front of us in the plane, eating and drinking.

In the shoe cupboard of his apartment in Monte Carlo, there are two pairs of cowboy boots: one black, one brown. He bought them in Dallas

BORIS OFF COURT

This Boris also exists, although it's impossible to imagine him without tennis. But here are a few scenes showing him without a racket in his hand.

I was very excited when we were invited to the White House in April. Before occasions like that, I almost lose my voice, I fiddle around endlessly with my jacket, comb my hair. We drove through Washington in two black Cadillacs: Ion and Vilas in front, Boris and I behind. As one of the iron White House gates opened and we were a few minutes away from being face to face with the Foreign Secretary of the United States of America, Boris suddenly ruffled my hair.

'Are you crazy?' I exploded. I couldn't find my comb. 'Boris, stop it!'

The Cadillac stopped. 'Boris, stop it, will you?'

Boris, who knows my hair is my weak spot, was killing himself laughing. I always made sure my hair was cut well, especially in situations like that. Sometimes I could really ...

On such occasions, Boris is the least excited of any of us. Foreign Secretary Schultz led us into the Oval Office and showed us the ministers' conference table. Boris sat down on a secretary's chair ... Later, on the White House tennis court, he yelled at Schultz, his doubles partner, 'Come on, run, you'll get it.' When Schultz reached the ball, Boris said, 'Very good, man.'

I stood at the edge of the court and wished the ground would open and swallow me up. 'You can't call Mr Schultz "man"...' But apparently he can, people take to him.

At the Wimbledon Finals, he winked at the German President in the Royal Box ... and the President winked back. At times like this, I nearly have a heart attack – and so do his parents.

Boris off court is like Boris on court.

At the celebration dinner afterwards in the Savoy, he chatted half the night with the Duchess of Kent. While the rest of us – even Martina Navratilova – sat fairly stiffly at the top table, Boris and the Duchess talked about surfing and cooking without meat (the Duchess is a vegetarian). Together with her, Boris developed his winner's address: 'Your Royal Highness, what should I say next?' They laughed; they liked each other.

At times like this, Boris is a stranger to me. He goes much further than I would. Never in a million years could I do what he does.

A year ago, when he won Wimbledon for the first time, Ion showed him how to bow before a 'Royal Highness'; which side of a lady a gentleman should stand on ... With his mother, he practised a few waltz steps in his hotel room. As far as we were concerned, the old tradition still stood that the winner of the mens' singles asked the winner of the ladies' singles for the first dance.

Boris's appearance when relaxed: his hand over his head, laughing to himself

He didn't have to ask Martina Navratilova, though: the old custom had been abolished. Since 1985, there was now just the dinner, no dance.

Journalists wrote that Boris was a glamour boy whose hotel was besieged by girls in all weathers, looking for a glimpse of that 'strawberry blond' (*Newsweek*) or 'carrot-red' (*Sports Illustrated*) hair. And, when he won the Junior Masters Tournament in Berlin the year before, an old lady had thrown her crutches away and hobbled across the court to present him with a rose. 'Good grief!' said Ulrich Kaiser the journalist, 'it was almost like being at Lourdes!'

The journalists call it 'like being at Lourdes'; Ion calls it charisma. Well, I still see him as the boy who ruffled my hair on the way to the White House. But maybe I'm too close to him to be impressed.

Sometimes, when we're alone, he shocks me.

'Wow, what if we went into the wall.' (This was at the wheel of his black Mercedes, with me in the passenger seat, coming back from a training session.)

Boris: That would be it then, wouldn't it?
Me: Stop talking rubbish.
Boris: Are you afraid of dying?
Me: Yes.
Boris: I'm not.
Me: Your life's just beginning.
Boris: If I died, I wouldn't know what I was missing.
Me: Don't talk rubbish.
Boris: What do you mean, rubbish?
Me: Slow down a bit.

With a dress on, Martina Navratilova is enchanting. At the celebration dinner after his second win at Wimbledon, Boris addressed Martina in his speech. 'I wish you many more wins at Wimbledon; because when you win, I win too.' Martina won at Wimbledon in '85 and '86 like Boris

154

Boris: I don't know what I'm missing. Why should I be afraid? You've got a daughter. I don't know what it's like to have a daughter.

I know by now that death is always present in his head. Perhaps I'm too old to understand the fascination that death can have for young people.

His hero is James Dean. Above his bed there is a poster for the film *Rebel Without A Cause*. He loves *East of Eden*, *Giant* and, of course, *Rebel Without A Cause*. He's got them on tape. The only books he's bought himself are biographies of James Dean. Each time we're in America, he wants to visit that crossroads in California where Dean died in an accident in his silver Porsche. Sometimes I think we ought to visit it and get it over with, so that he can see there is nothing mysterious about it, that it's just a normal crossroads where there was an accident.

By now, as I write this, I think, 'What rubbish. We'll never go there. Rubbish ...'

There's a place in Monte Carlo where Boris likes to go at night: a quayside near the marina. The stone where he sits and looks out at the sea is still warm from the sun. He can sit for hours on that stone.

I'm not saying there is anything unusual about that: there are many youngsters sitting on similar stones, thinking the same thing as they gaze out to sea: 'What's the world like, what am I doing here?'

Boris often asks me, 'You're married. What's that like?' Or: 'You've got a daughter. What's it like when you see her?' Or: 'When do you think a man should get married?'

'At twenty-nine.' I don't know why I said twenty-nine.

When his parents entrusted him to my care he was a fifteen-year-old boy. I don't just feel responsible for his tennis. I don't want him to end up like Borg, burnt out and broken after his career. Separated at twenty-nine, empty ...

Ion says Boris will never be poor.

I reply, 'That's not enough.' I think that perhaps winning at tennis is not the meaning of life, but it can be a foundation for later life. Borg's victories burnt him out. Now, there's no

Above: *Boris on a chat show. He likes this picture of himself. I'm not the only one who thinks he looks very much like his idol, James Dean, here*

Right: *Boris with Rodica, my wife, at a charity do in Berlin. Boris handed over a cheque for 120,000 marks for handicapped children. As his coach, I know: Boris's conscience often troubles him, because he has it good and, as he says, 'I've been so lucky in my life.'*

drive in his life. He's rich; but that's not enough. In my dreams, I see Boris – even at thirty or forty – showing people that it's always worth putting up a fight. I'd like him to be like Max Schmeling, the famous German boxer of the 1930s – an example.

When I told Boris about Schmeling, he protested.

'No way do I want to become a legend. I won't be a tennis player for ever.'

HALF TIME

'Boris off court' doesn't just laugh, mess around and chat with celebrities; he has also had to struggle: this was at the time when he didn't know whether he was a grown-up or a child.

That was a bad time: it was at Flushing Meadow a year ago, playing against Nystrom and then against Pernfors in Paris. 'A start in life,' the Americans say. Beginning to live, changing from a boy to a man. It was a terrible struggle. Flushing Meadow, a year ago, was when his conflicts and self-castigation were at their height. When he shouted at the world on the Centre Court, 'I'm a child, I can't take it any more ...', then, the next moment, 'No, I'm a man.'

There is one image of this child-man I will never forget: after losing at Flushing Meadow, he was lying on the massage table and beating the equipment with his fists, crying and shouting, 'I want to beat him, I want to beat him!' A strange picture, those 'howling fists' ...

A year after his second defeat at Flushing Meadow (against Mecir in the semi-finals), Boris was completely different. He was furious with himself, sore – one wrong word and ...! –

but there was no letting himself go, no flipping out, no howling around. He had learnt to take defeat.

The change to being a man had happened. We went around together as adults: everyone in the team, and everyone around it. His mother, his father. The 'in between' time had passed – I was happy that we were still the same. The team was still there, Boris had reached number two. He had overtaken Wilander in the world ratings.

In Paris, Boris was still a minor. I didn't know how to go on. The match against Pernfors was something I couldn't understand. I've already mentioned that match: I'd never seen Boris 'tank', give up. The word comes from the tennis professionals: they've twisted the idea of being like a tank, crushing everything in its path – a 'tanker' is someone who gives up. Boris had 'tanked', given up, stopped fighting – even if he didn't see it that way. He'd never lost a set 0-6 before.

In Paris, I threw up my hands. When we trained, he was aggressive, raging, shouting – there were times when I thought, 'That's it as far as we're concerned.' It was worse than in Dallas. Dallas was just a preview. In Paris, there was no making up like there was in Dallas. As I write about growing up, I can see a scene with his mother before my eyes: I'd rung her up from Paris and said, 'Please come.'

Frau Becker rang back and got through to my wife.

I was in Boris's room; my wife came in and said, 'Boris, your mother will be here at two.'

A glimpse inside. Boris just before serving: eyes half closed, mouth open, total concentration

'Why, how come?' His face was scornful. 'I see, my mother's coming to comfort me.'

He was a child again.

I ought to say at this point that Boris is very attached to his mother: whenever he's in Leimen for a day (such as when he was made an honorary citizen, for instance), they both find it difficult to say goodbye.

'Your mother's not coming because you're a little kid,' I said. 'She's coming because she's your mother. She needs to see you.'

Boris: 'I don't understand. I'm no mother.'

He says things like that sometimes, trying to play it cool.

Three hours later, his mother arrived.

I was still reeling from the Pernfors disaster. There were the three of us in his hotel room.

'There's no one who wishes you luck more than your parents and your sister,' I said. 'As your trainer, I can only come so close, but there's no comparison between that and the feeling a father or mother has for their son. Nor the feeling you have as a son for your parents. If you won't tell me, tell your mother.'

I was convinced Boris was no 'tanker'. There had to be something inside him, something he wouldn't tell me. The only thing to do was to get it out.

I left the room. What kind of a coach was I?

I don't think it helps if you tell your player, 'Now play the forehand this way ...' or, 'You should have used your knees more, you should have got to it earlier ...' or, 'Run faster, get stuck in more, be more positive, more aggressive.'

That's not coaching. In my opinion, the technical, tactical and conditional ability in a player like Boris only works when the inner motor is running properly.

That's all a long way in the past now. It all happened before Wimbledon II, before Flushing Meadow. Everyone asked how he could win the second time at Wimbledon so calmly, how he could make himself so positive: the same at Stratton Mountain, Toronto, and the semi-finals at Flushing Meadow.

As far as I'm concerned, it all began in Paris.

I wasn't there when he talked with his mother; they'd gone out for a walk together. The next day, Boris was – I won't say 'changed', but more confident. He told Ion Tiriac what he wanted and what he didn't want. He could express himself, he didn't use emotional arguments, he said what he meant clearly and concisely.

The little things he talks about in this book – driving on his own, going round cities on his own, getting stuck in a jam, being with people whose minds aren't just on tennis – those are the outward signs.

To put it in a nutshell, what he told us was, 'I don't want to be your kid any more.' He could also have said 'puppet'.

As I saw Boris standing there in front of Ion, it gave me so much motivation as a trainer that I said: 'So now I'll give up everything, all my thoughts, day and night. We'll get through it. It'll all get sorted out.'

There was a total change in the organization, in his life, which was over-organized, where the human element had been neglected; it was all too much tennis, nothing but tennis.

Of course, tennis was still the main thing. You don't get anywhere without working. No training, no success.

But where does that success get you? Now I was coming to the important point. And here, I'm in opposition to Ion and many other trainers. For me, the emphasis is not on training the weaknesses but the strengths. In Paris, we were training Boris's weaknesses. In Ion's luxury hide-away club, we were sparring with shadows.

That was enough.

Since Boris had the courage to say he didn't want to go on living that way, I've only trained

A typical Ion Tiriac gesture: with four fingers, he explains how he was cunning and tricky as a player

his strengths. The first thing, though, was to get back the joy in life.

At the Queens warm-up tournament for Wimbledon II, he flew to Monte Carlo on his own for two days. He had an inflamed tendon in his serving hand. The tournament doctor had recommended two days' rest. He had an anti-inflammation cream which he was supposed to apply morning, noon and night. It didn't matter where he took the break, in England or at home

The new face of Boris. On court, Boris was a man at sixteen: now, at eighteen, he can be one off it as well. He's no longer a minor

in Monte Carlo. I sensed he wanted to be back home in his apartment.

'Get lost,' I said. Three days later, he came back, happy, his hand healed.

He came back wanting to win. He'd booked the flight himself, picked up the keys to his flat from the porter in Monte Carlo, gone shopping for food, made himself coffee. He'd arranged for an early morning alarm call, because he had to be up at 5.30 the next morning.

He was ready to play tennis.

Little things? Big things to a boy who couldn't have any phone calls put through to him during tournaments, who had bodyguards, was driven around by chauffeurs, who had to pretend that a girl he liked was a friend of my daughter's or his sister, so that the press didn't make her life a misery. 'Who's she, what's she got? Where did it start? Is it true love or just cupboard love?'

From now on, we would only train his strengths. His service, mainly, linked with service fly balls, then returns, keeping the other player under pressure all the time ... the pressure game.

A boxer preparing for a world championship fight doesn't train with opponents who are his equals. He looks for sparring partners he can reduce to rubble. The only players I looked for for Boris's training sessions were weak ones, a different one every time. The idea was for him to wipe them off the court, bombard them with aces ...

Of course he won't get his service 100 per cent right that way; but his self-confidence will increase, and then, when he really is up against a proper opponent, a better opponent than those sparring partners, then it will carry over into the match. That's what I think – that's what I hope.

Once, Ion came to me. 'He's not getting any returns, he'll have to do half an hour of returns tomorrow.'

We didn't. Nor did I tell Boris he wasn't getting any returns. Why should I? He noticed it himself.

His rebellion in the process of growing up was not just directed against the 'fine' hotels, the life of luxury. It was directed against the lack of freedom on court; against being patronized.

If you emphasize what is bad, the crisis eats its way into your head and stays there. It can cause a real psychosis: a player can become mentally ill. 'My return, my return ...' He gets into a state of panic. Instead of things getting better, they get worse.

This is a basic mistake in tennis: trainers train faults.

We were coming up to Wimbledon – 'the spectre of Wimbledon'. We were training for self-confidence and our priorities were service, returns too of course, but without harping on them, and fly balls. Those are the decisive factors on grass. You can train for the feeling of winning, the optimism to win.

Nowadays I'm a coach who trains weaknesses in strokes with great diplomacy, very carefully. Take Boris's backhand. A catastrophic weakness one day may turn out to be your greatest strength the next. With the Top Ten, strokes are like the hunter's shots: it has to involve the humidity of the air, the light, your own feelings, the movement of the quarry, hair-trigger equipment faults, all these kind of things.

Playing ability grows as a player develops as a human being. Why does no one like Lendl? Because he doesn't enjoy his game. He doesn't 'live' it. The spectators sense this; his cold game leaves them cold.

If Boris plays tennis without enjoying it, he loses. If he doesn't enjoy life, he doesn't enjoy playing. I don't mean the high life or anything like that: as a professional, he has no high life. He'd be down to number 50 in six months.

What makes him happy is to be able to say to Ion or me, 'Right, I'm going to disappear.'

What makes him happy is that his parents no longer say, 'You have to do this' or 'You have to do that' or 'Watch out, watch where you're going.'

What makes him happy is the fact that we trust him.

No one makes his decisions for him any more. The second half has begun.

COACHING

'No coaching is allowed during a tournament match. Any player breaking this rule will receive a warning, then lose points, then games, and finally be disqualified. Players themselves are responsible for any action on the part of their coaches.' (From the official professional tournament rules.)

They say Boris and I have a secret language. British reporters were out to prove it. They photographed me at Wimbledon for a whole week; then they published all the photo sequences and under each picture they wrote what my eyes, my forehead, my hands were 'saying'. In one picture, I had my hand over my eyes because of the sun: that was supposed to mean 'net attack'. I laughed myself silly.

Yes, I coach. But not by scratching my ear or turning my head one way or the other. In the 'high' Boris is in when he's playing, the emotional state he's in, he wouldn't even notice thinks like that. What he does notice are signs of feelings, not my left earlobe, which the reporters claim means, 'Play to the backhand'.

Coaching. We watch how the other players move, how they hit the ball. What they're like when they make mistakes: whether they get sore, or hide it. This is what's called 'getting the opponent's scent before a match'

Now, in the semi-final in Flushing Meadow against Miroslav Mecir, Boris signalled to me, 'Coach, he serves like my mother, that's a housewife's serve. I can't play against someone like that.'

Boris didn't shout this to me; with his racket, he showed me Mecir's housewife's service.

Mecir is a run-of-the-mill player, inconspicuous, versatile ... We weren't underestimating him. One of the most difficult games at Wimbledon II was the quarter-final against Mecir ... Boris won it in three sets, 6-4, 6-2, 7-6.

That might sound easy, but it was a game of nerves. Mecir is unpredictable, his service is soft ... He fishes everything out with his long 'kraken arm', as the press calls it. [A kraken was a legendary sea monster of gigantic size believed to dwell off the coast of Norway.]

Coaching?

Coaching begins the evening before a match. Over our meal, Boris and I talk about the other player. Boris has already played Mecir a few times. In Rotterdam a year ago, he didn't stand a chance against him: 'the average man' played perfectly, won the tournament, and we both said, 'Hats off to him!' In the Davis Cup in Germany, Boris wiped the court with him ... Mecir is a maniac, unpredictable in the positive sense of the word. Once, against Connors, he seemed to lose his nerve, served underarm, and played the ball across the net like children do when they're just starting to play tennis.

We know Mecir well. Eighteen months ago, we saw him in Philadelphia; there, too, he got as

far as the Finals. Boris and I were sitting in the players' lounge. Mecir drank a cup of tea quietly in the corner, and then, without warming himself up, he went out on to the court with his cup of tea still in his hand, put it down somewhere and played the match. We'd never seen anything like it.

After a ball change, he moved like an old man, you'd think he was asleep on his feet. Not a sign of aggression, not the slightest will to win. He's 'crazy'.

What Boris was 'shouting' up to me was, 'He's not playing tennis. How can I play against him?'

I replied, 'Play the ball further in, more into the court, don't go all the way.'

We were at Flushing Meadow. Three years ago, two years ago, a year ago, we'd been in New York. You can't imagine what it's like. Boris is a hero in America. Three years ago, no one would have given us a second look. Now ...

For Boris, it was a home match. Twenty thousand people in the stadium. The planes from nearby La Guardia airport thundered over the Centre Court. It was an American national festival: 'Boris is playing, Boris Becker ...'

Everyone wanted to see him in the Final against Lendl. They all wanted him to beat Lendl. That was the New Yorkers' greatest wish. You could feel it at any hamburger joint.

Scornful of Mecir's 'housewife's serve', Boris smashed the ball at him – always three or four centimetres behind the line. He went mad. In Boris's mind, Mecir was serving 'plumb crazy'. Boris's service grew to resemble Mecir's. Eleven double faults; only 60 per cent of his services worked.

Mecir returned all his shots.

Boris lost the match 6-4, 3-6, 4-6, 6-3, 3-6.

Bad coaching? Obviously.

Would it have been good coaching if he'd won?

If you lose, you're nothing. Even in Ion's eyes, I could see the reproach: bad coaching.

I'd been unable to convince Boris during that stupid game. I thought he could win the match; we wrestled with one another the whole way through. He would say to me, 'I can't play someone who isn't playing tennis …'

I would reply, 'Forget him, play your normal game.'

I lost. I should have been stronger than Boris. It really choked me. I've never told him how much something like that kills me. I couldn't sleep afterwards.

At the press conference, Boris said that he couldn't adjust to Mecir's game, but it wouldn't kill him. I was standing four steps behind him, with pains in my stomach.

I'm not coaching if I indicate to Boris, 'Now forehand, now backhand.' All these signs, these secret signals everyone writes about – it's all

Occupation: tennis player. Boris's everyday job. Jogging before breakfast, three hours' training each morning, three hours each afternoon. At 11 at night, in a restaurant somewhere, Boris says, 'Coach, I fancy a bit of tennis.' Sometimes he picks up a racket as if to ease his conscience. It's an obsessional occupation

Overleaf: *Boris's place of work. He lies on the grass, feeling as if he's hidden. Those are my legs behind him*

167

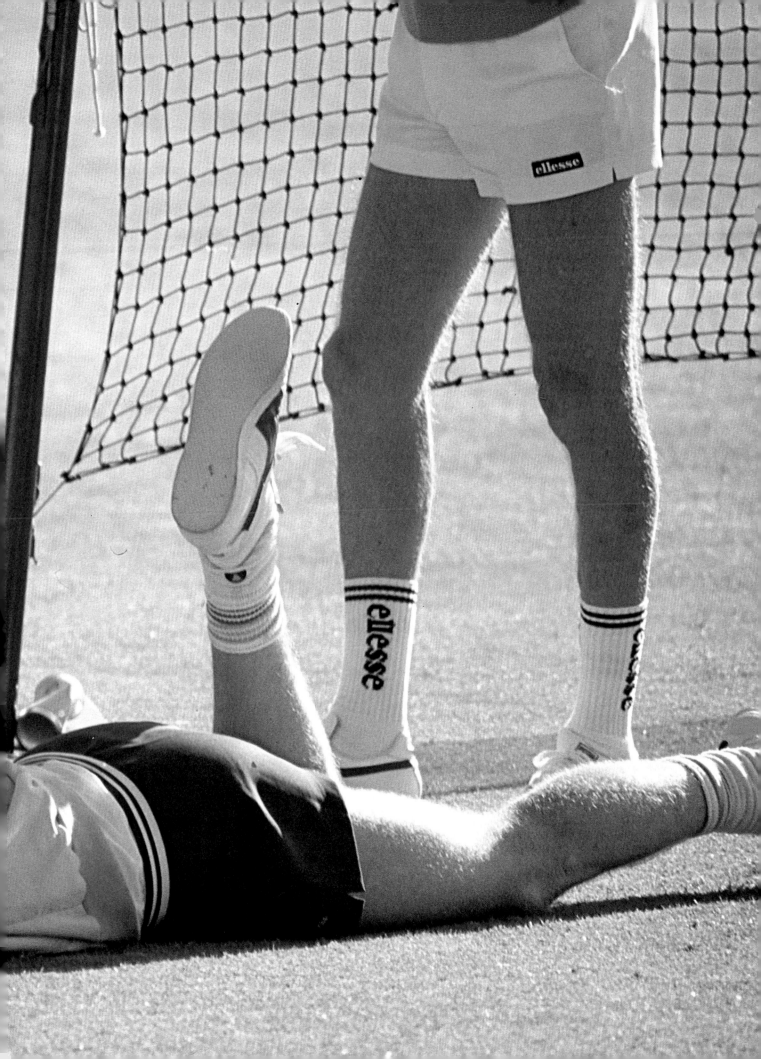

rubbish. How can I explain? The coaching begins – began, rather, when I first started training Boris.

He was fifteen years old, he played a ball, looked up – I nodded. How many hours of training have passed since then? We know every hint in each other's face, every hand movement, every gesture. He can read my face and I can read his.

By breakfast time we usually know how the match will go that afternoon. We can't hide anything from each other by now: we only have to look in each other's eyes to see what's up.

'Careful,' I tell Ion or people sitting near us. 'Leave us in peace. Leave us alone.'

Even before that match with the 'impossible' Mecir, we could feel it, downstairs at the breakfast buffet in the St Regis Sheraton Hotel. It's a beautiful old hotel, recently renovated: the view was impressive looking down on Fifth Avenue from our windows on the 14th floor.

Playing Mecir and playing Lendl are two different pressure situations. The pressure was much stronger with Mecir.

Mecir, the crazy tea-drinker and angler (he takes his fishing gear to tournaments and fishes any stream he can find), is someone you have to beat. It's having to that's the pressure.

You can beat Lendl: the pressure is much less.

The weaker a player, the greater the inner pressure. You can try and hide it, but we can't hide it from each other. We could tell it wouldn't be easy. But what could we do?

A player like Boris doesn't need any sophisticated technique. The problem is Boris – not Mecir. Boris is his own programme: his service, the thrust of his strokes, his return, his forehand, his will to win.

But what if his service won't come? Tug my

Wimbledon Finals 1986. Ion and I. Next to Ion, Jerry Solomin from ProServ, Lendl's manager. The third set: Lendl has three set points against Boris. Boris pulls back. Jerry's face says it all

left earlobe? Put my right hand on my left arm to get him to play to the other man's forehand?

It's all rubbish. My coaching lies in the fact that indirectly I'm there playing too, and Boris can feel it. He knows I'm there fighting along with him for every point.

In the match against Mecir, my whole body language, my gestures, my whole body was saying, 'Don't risk so much, not all or nothing, play the ball more into the court, don't play to the edge, don't play it to the line.'

I was sitting in the stands in my tracksuit. The fact that I had my training suit on told him I was sweating with him. It's our working gear. 'You're working out there,' Boris says, 'I'm working down here.' Although I can't do his running or hitting for him, we're as one.

If you like, that in itself means I'm infringing Article 31 of the International Tennis Federation which says that players must not be assisted physically or psychologically. I coach Boris by wearing my tracksuit. He can see me amongst all the ties and pullovers, wearing 'his' clothes – working, fighting, sweating. He's not alone.

Perhaps the next thing the ITF will do is ban all fathers, mothers, wives and friends from sitting in the stands – after all, aren't they giving the players moral support?

But the umpires and journalists who've been watching me like hawks since Wimbledon I aren't concerned with things like that. They're trying to find the secret because they still can't believe it's Boris down there on court.

No eighteen-year-old can beat Lendl, win Wimbledon twice, or get to number two in the world. There must be a secret to it somewhere, a trick.

Now they won't let us out of their sight. Every gesture, every nod is immediately 'coaching' and banned. On that basis, there isn't a single player who doesn't get coached from the sidelines. Even Lendl. You can't look up much more clearly than Navratilova did to her coach Mike Estep in Paris.

I had hoped that Rule 31 would be altered this spring. You don't have a football match without a coach, a boxing match without a coach, a

basketball match without a coach. But the bid to change the rules was squashed: the penalties were even increased.

First it's 'First warning, coaching, Mr Becker.' Then 'Second warning, Mr Becker.' Then Boris loses a point, then a whole game. Finally, a fine is imposed: if it's more than 7500 dollars, the player is banned for 43 days. The fine for coaching is added to the fine for throwing your racket around or insulting the umpire.

It's crazy.

Just imagine: the score is 30-40. A break. 'Second warning, coaching, Mr Becker.' He loses the point. He loses the game.

I've asked Boris, 'What are we going to do? Every time you play, the umpire's looking me in the eye.'

Boris: 'I'll get the point back. Don't let it annoy you.'

I'm not saying this for Boris's sake or mine. It's tennis as a whole that's suffering. I'm con-

Doubles pair No. 1: Boris and 'Bobo'. They're amongst the Top Ten world doubles pairs. Slobodan Zivojinovic is also managed by Ion. Bobo has a baby: when Bobo is training, Boris babysits

vinced players would be much more disciplined if their official coach could bring an appeal. Say a ball is on the line, but is given 'out'. Boris looks at me. I'm not allowed to say a thing. He protests, gets worked up, loses his touch, the game deteriorates. Wouldn't it be better if I could go to the umpire?

Doubles pair No. 2: Meeting on the Centre Court: Boris, men's number two in the world, and Chris Evert-Lloyd, ladies' number two. Her career is nearing its end, Boris's is just beginning

Wouldn't it be better for tennis?

There's another example: Bjorn Borg. But I don't want him being another Borg.

Bjorn Borg, the iceberg. Borg is the supreme god of tennis, the inscrutable father of the gods. How did he manage it? By never enjoying himself, never getting cross, always being in control – without any help from outside. A thousand tournaments, without any feeling ...

Many people have tried to play like him. They have all failed. No one knows how he did it. No outbreak of nerves, no reaction. Five times he won Wimbledon, six times Paris: you can't win more than that.

I know from Mariana, his wife, now separated, who was my pupil in Romania, that she couldn't get behind the mask either.

Borg would sit in the players' lounge, never speak to anyone, drink his Coke, stare at the wall. Before a match, he used to warm up with his wife. He didn't need anyone else to warm up with; no player was his equal: it was just to warm up a bit, to get warm.

A real riddle. In the stands sat Bergelin, his coach. Borg never looked up at him. Maybe, after the winning ball, there was the hint of a smile. After his fourth win at Wimbledon, he fell

173

to his knees and made as if to thank God; the same thing happened after his fifth win. His hands up in the air, his face towards heaven.

Borg – this is my theory – was destroyed by his own self-discipline. It wasn't human.

After Boris's second win at Wimbledon, we went through what would happen in an emergency. What if Boris was due to play a match, and I fell ill and couldn't make it? There were three of us talking: Boris, myself and a reporter who is our friend. We recorded the conversation on tape.

Reporter: Boris, won't you have to train sometimes to play on your own? I mean, your coach might have to go into hospital suddenly – an appendix operation, maybe ...
Me: I've already had it out.
Reporter: OK, your tonsils ... but Boris still has to play. It's a real emergency, flashing blue lights, the lot ... Wouldn't Boris then have to play the match on his own, without you?
Boris, to me: Has that ever occurred to you?
Me: Let me think about it first.
Boris: Well, I think I'd notice how valuable you are ... [he stretches his arm behind his head and fidgets in his chair]. It's like a wife ... The moment you lose her, for whatever reason, only then do you notice how important she was, how much she helped.

The Davis Cup: last warming-up session before the first match of the Finals against Mats Wilander. We are sitting in the Olympiahalle. Boris looks at the court one more time, getting his eyes used to the light. The stands are still empty: the TV crews are putting their cameras up. Inside Boris, a mixture of many moods: aggression, impatience, the lust to win, and uncertainty

Me: What do you know about wives?

Boris: Or parents ...

Me: God forbid that such a thing should ever happen. But if I really had to lie there, and Boris had a match ... if I could see from my window that he was in trouble ... I'd leap out of bed and run to the court, never mind the consequences. I'd do a bunk from the hospital. I'd be itching so much; I couldn't bear it. I don't think the experiment would work. Maybe we could do it in training, try it, perhaps. No, my conscience wouldn't let me. Could you do it, Boris?

Boris: In training, yes.

Me: When people ask you questions like that, you think, 'Well, you'd better make sure the situation doesn't occur when you're lying in bed.'

Boris: Have you ever missed a match of mine in the last three years?

Me: No.

Boris: Coach, we'll include it in our training.

Dialogue with a racket: Boris's face radiates happiness. It went well. He picks at the strings. A good shot. He straightens them. It's like tuning an instrument: the racket is like an extension of his arm. Boris says his rackets are alive

176

BORIS WAKES UP

As a boy, Boris dreamt of Vilas and Borg. Ion and I dreamt of food, of finally having enough to eat. The war was on. When I was training Boris at fourteen, sometimes a flash of his dreams would show through: 'There, that was a Borg return ...'

Now I hear children on tennis courts shouting, 'I'll be Boris, you be Lendl!'

Four or five years ago, Boris was a kid like them: he would sit in front of the TV in Leimen: Wimbledon – Borg v. Connors, Borg v. McEnroe. Then suddenly, there he was, winning there twice himself – twice ...

How many children dream of that? How many now dream of Boris and say, 'Man, if only I could do what Boris did. It must be incredible, the way he feels.'

Sometimes, to keep Boris's feet on the ground, I go back with him over the way we've come, the rocky road on which so many kids founder: the daily practice sessions on court, pushing yourself harder and harder, not giving up, brushing off defeat, believing in yourself.

Boris wasn't like Tore Meinecke from Hamburg, who announced at the age of fifteen, 'I'm

The match is over: the winning shot. Boris stretches his fist up to me. That's our sign: it's become a ritual. It means, 'Work's over. Let's go home, coach.'

going to win Wimbledon.' Boris had dreamt of doing it: but to actually say it out loud ...

Boris looked up to Tore because he was the number one in their age group, and Boris was number four. But who won Wimbledon? The number four! Boris got into the DTB training scheme in twenty-second place; somehow, I managed to smuggle him in. And now he is where he is today.

Two years ago, when he pulled out of Wimbledon with a torn ligament, I sat by his bed the whole night. That was in Munich, where he was being operated on. He didn't want any anaesthetic because he can't stand injections. He was like an animal. After the operation the surgeon told me, 'We had to put your player in a cage.'

After the operation, they put him in a room with other patients who'd just had operations; but he thrashed around like a wild beast, until they had to put cot-sides around his bed: he would have smashed everything up otherwise. He was then brought semi-conscious to his room, where I was waiting for him. He raged around, tried to tear his plaster off, smash his leg to pieces. I forced his hand behind his back. I didn't know what else I could do. Call the doctor? The sister? 'No pain-killers, no pain-killers!'

In his delirium, he cried, 'Massage me, hold my leg up!' Probably his circulation wasn't very good when he was lying down. I held his leg up, massaged it and massaged it, all day.

But then, when the pain became unbearable, he finally accepted some drugs. Doctors don't

force people to take them. They put up a drip; the pain eased off.

Hardly had the first drip-bottle nearly emptied when he was screaming for the next. The pain had been so great, he was panic-stricken at the thought it might come back.

I went through his suffering with him. OK, I slept at the hotel, but I was at his bedside each day until the evening. We got ourselves a television: after all, Wimbledon was still going on, and we saw McEnroe win.

They let Boris out of hospital with his leg in plaster. Two days later, he was training again – still with the plaster on. I played the balls to him, he played them back. He couldn't walk: he could only stand there and hit the ball.

When we think back to that time, he is amazed. It's like waking up from a dream.

'What, two years ago I was number 476 on the computer ranking list?'

When I look at his face, he really looks as if he's been woken from his sleep. 'What was I dreaming about?'

And he remembers: 'Once, you made me go without my dinner. We were on Majorca, the training camp ... Do you still remember, Guntzi? Our old quartet ... The others were in my room with me, I was telling them some story, and we missed our dinner. We should have eaten at 7.30. At 8 o'clock, suddenly you were there in

---

The next book about us as a team will be written by Boris himself. I'll help him with it if he wants, the same way as he helped me. His memory amazes me: he can recite all his scores from memory, picture every scene, name any date. He writes down things which have nothing to do with tennis: his own private life

the room. 'No dinner for anyone. Take it up with Boris.' I was so cross! In the night, I went down to the hotel kitchens, I wanted to get something together for the others. Everything was locked up. I was so cross with you, I wouldn't speak to you for the rest of the week. We were awake at 5 the next morning, our stomachs were rumbling so much. At that time, I'd just become the number one in the group. You said, 'Number one is responsible ... I was still calling you "Herr Bosch" at the time; I only started calling you "Guntzi" like your wife does just before Wimbledon.'

That was three years ago. That year, Boris was nineteen.

After losing at Flushing Meadow, he said, 'I'll just stay one more day.'

'OK, Boris, I'll go to Monte Carlo on my own. We have to be in Hamburg on Thursday – you know, the German International Championships at Rothenbaum.'

'OK, coach,' he said.

Ion's management had booked us hotel rooms in Hamburg; we would meet there. Boris would call me in my room. 'Everything OK?'

I'm glad that's how it is between us. It's been that way since Paris. Boris has fought his way free.

At Wimbledon, I could sense it on the court too. He stood on court self-confident. He won the tournament with self-confidence. Now he's starting to pick me up on things. 'Hey, coach, what do you look like? What kind of shirt is that you've got on?' And he finds me another shirt. 'And always that leather jacket ...'

In New York, he turned up one day with some theatre tickets. 'Coach, we're going to see *A Chorus Line*.'

'Where?' I had no idea what he was talking about.

It was impressive to see how the dancers there fought for their careers ... But for Boris, I would never have seen it.

His parents came over: Boris took them around, showed them New York, acted as interpreter. He did it quite unobtrusively. I'm glad he gets on so well with his parents.

Boris has grown up – I'm not afraid any more.

POSTSCRIPT

Günther Bosch chose 21 January 1987, the day after Boris Becker had been eliminated from the Australian Open in Melbourne by the unseeded Wally Masur, to announce that he was no longer prepared to work with the young West German: that he was to leave the tight coterie of advisers who had dictated the course of Becker's career.

It was apparent that though the divorce was something to regret there also was relief. Bosch told reporters who besieged his room as he finished breakfast: 'I have put a lot of thought into this decision. Boris no longer has the right attitude. There is no way back for me. It is impossible for me to co-operate with him. Our opinions on the way he should prepare for matches, the tournaments in which he should play and other circumstances which surround these matters are incompatible.'

Bosch's decision did not entirely astonish the world of tennis. As far back as the United States Open – in which Becker, surprisingly, had been defeated by the Czech Miroslav Mecir in the semi-finals – journalists who covered the professional circuit had detected growing conflict between the player and his coach.

Becker had left Melbourne before Bosch's announcement but, subsequently, he said he could hardly believe Bosch was no longer his coach. They had had their problems, the young man explained, but he never thought they would part. On the other hand, he was at pains to stress that he would not try and persuade Bosch to change his mind. Becker's father, Karl-Heinz,

was less surprised. He had seen smoke in the kitchen but thought the fire would be extinguished!

It seemed there had been two causes of the smoke. The first was that Becker, secure in his fame and investments and increasingly independent, had suggested that Bosch should only accompany him to some tournaments, something with which Bosch vehemently disagreed. 'That is not good enough for me. I must have continuity. If he goes to a tournament at Indian Wells and I arrive next week at Key Biscayne as he suggested, how will I know how his backhand has been working? How will I know what needs to be done? I cannot work like that.'

'Personally, we are fine,' Bosch explained shortly after he had made public his decision. 'Boris the tennis player is still developing and Boris the man, too. I think he still needs someone with him.'

The second cause of the smoke was that the young West German did, indeed, have someone with him. Tension had been surfacing within the Becker camp since the Wimbledon champion had started travelling with his girlfriend, Benedicte Courtin, daughter of a Monte Carlo government official. Becker explained: 'Benedicte helps me. It's not very easy after a strong and hard day's training to come back to your apartment and be alone. You are tired and not always in the best shape. It is so much better to come back somewhere when there is a nice person sitting there to cheer you up and to offer encouragement.'

According to some commentators, Bosch

neither accepted Mlle Courtin nor that times were changing. Ion Tiriac explained: 'Boris was very hurt by Bosch and only when you are hurt do you find out how much of a man you are.' Bosch and Tiriac had been friends since growing up together in Romania. After Bosch's decision that friendship, sadly, became strained. Tiriac said: 'I don't understand Bosch at all. As far as I am concerned, he betrayed not me but Boris. He didn't have that right. Boris made him and my company paid him in gold. As a coach you must have integrity, loyalty and fidelity. Bosch has shown he didn't have any of these qualities.'

Ultimately, it had become an acrimonious break-up. Perhaps Rod Laver, four times Wimbledon champion, summed it up as well as anyone. 'The truth,' he said, 'is that Boris Becker is growing up. He probably doesn't need a full-time coach any more, just somebody to give him an occasional pat on the back.'

All the same, it was a sad end to a partnership that was conquering the world. Boris would now try his luck with Frank Dick, the coach of British decathlete Daley Thompson. At least he could look forward to defending his Wimbledon title with the help of Britain's finest athletics coach.

Michael Herd
March 1987

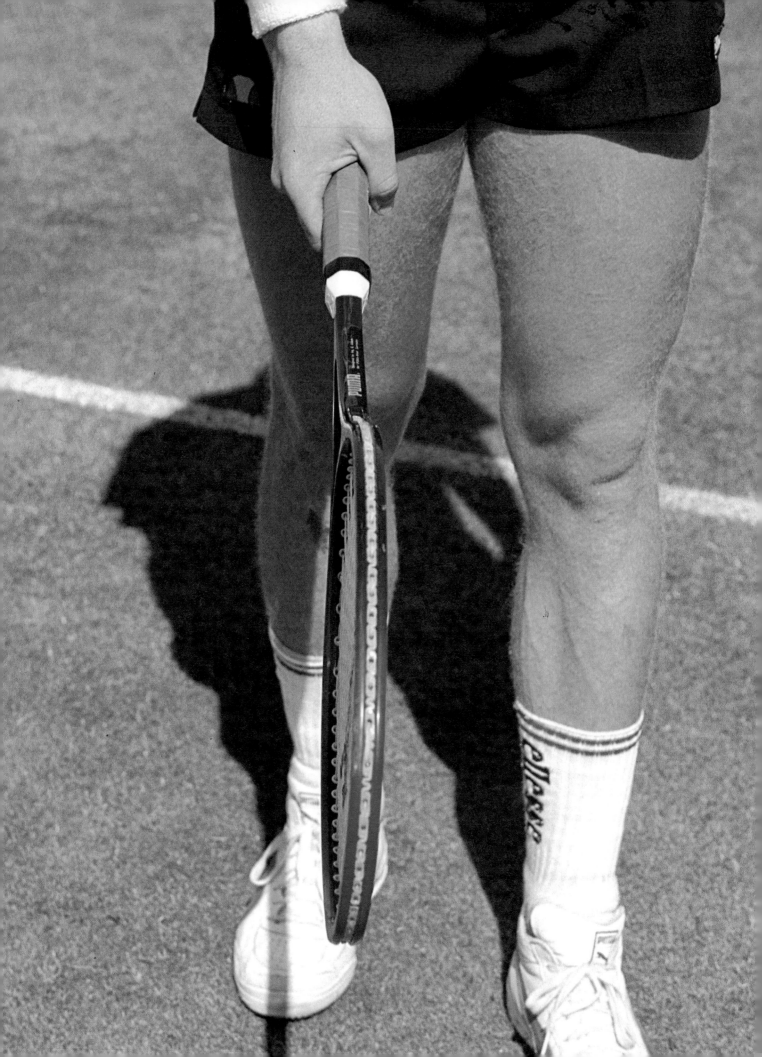

BORIS BECKER

Born: 22 November 1967
Place of birth: Leimen
Height: 1.90 m (6 ft 2 ins)
Weight: 82 kg (12 st 9 lbs)
Racket: Puma Boris Becker Super
Strings: Vollmer
String tension: 28 kg (61.7 lbs)
Clothes: Puma (previously ellesse)
Shoes: Puma
Other sponsors: Deutsche Bank, Philips,
Coca-Cola, Ebel

World position (at end of each year):
1983: 476
1984: 65
1985: 6
1986: 2

Tournament wins (up to the end of 1986):
Young Masters (1985, 1986 and 1987 (played in
December 1986))
Queens (1985)
Wimbledon (1985 and 1986)
Cincinnati (1985)
Chicago (1986)
Toronto (1986)
Sydney (1986)
Tokyo (1986)
Paris (1986)
Atlanta (1986)

ALL MATCHES 1985

Young Masters (indoors), Birmingham
(2–6.1)
Becker–Bale (England)
6-2, 6-2
Becker–Krickstein (USA)
6-3, 6-1
Becker–R. Brown (USA)
6-3, 6-4
Becker–Giammalva (USA)
7-6, 6-3, 6-3
Becker–Edberg (Sweden)
4-6, 6-3, 6-1, 4-6, 6-3

Exhibition tournament, Portland
(10–14.1)
Becker–Weiss (USA)
6-0, 6-2
Becker–R. Leach (USA)
6-4, 6-0
Becker–Purcell (USA)
6-4, 6-4

Grand Prix tournament, Philadelphia
(21–27.1)
Singles:
Becker–Kuharszky (Hungary)
6-7, 6-4, 6-2
Becker–Edberg (Sweden)
3-6, 1-6
Doubles:
with Edberg (Sweden)–
Gonzalez/Motta
(Paraguay/Brazil)
7-6, 4-6, 6-4
with Edberg–
Dowlen/Odizor (USA/Nigeria)
6-3, 3-6, 4-6

Grand Prix tournament, Memphis
(28.1–3.2)
Singles:
Becker–Fibak (Poland)
6-2, 6-1
Becker–Smid (Czechoslovakia)
6-2, 6-4
Becker–Perkis (Israel)
6-4, 4-6, 4-6
Doubles:
with Maurer (West Germany)–
Acuna/Fernandez
(Chile/Puerto Rico)
6-4, 6-7, 6-3
with Maurer–
Gunthardt/Taroczy
(Switzerland/Hungary)
6-1, 6-1
with Maurer–
Curren/Denton (USA)
6-3, 4-6, 3-6

Grand Prix, Delray Beach
(5–17.2)
Singles:
Becker–Rive (USA)
6-2, 6-3
Becker–Mayotte (USA)
2-6, 3-6
Doubles:
with Fibak (Poland)–
Leach/Turpin (USA)
7-5, 6-3
with Fibak–
Dowlen/Odizor (USA/Nigeria)
7-6, 6-4
with Fibak–
Buehning/Taygan (USA)
4-6, 4-6
Mixed doubles:
with Kohde (West Germany)–
B. Cox/M. White (USA)
5-7, 6-4, 7-5
with Kohde–
Layendecker/Moulton (USA)
6-3, 6-4

Davis Cup: 1st round v. Spain 3-2
(8–10.3)
Singles:
Becker–Aguilera
6-3, 6-4, 6-4
Becker–Casal
4-6, 6-1, 5-7
Doubles:
with Maurer–
Casal/Sanchez
4-6, 6-3, 1-6, 6-3, 6-4

Grand Prix tournament, Brussels
(11–17.3)
Singles:
Becker–Green (USA)
7-6, 5-7, 6-4
Becker–Smid (Czechoslovakia)
7-5, 6-7, 5-7
Doubles:
with Lloyd (England)–
Edberg/Jarryd (Sweden)
7-5, 3-6, 4-6

Grand Prix tournament, Rotterdam
(18–24.3)
Singles:
Becker–Gerulaitis (USA)
6-2, 4-6, 7-6
Becker–Green (USA)
7-6, 6-0
Becker–Mecir
(Czechoslovakia)
4-6, 2-6

Doubles:
with Amritraj (India)–
Krishnan/Ostoja
(India/Yugoslavia)
6-7, 6-2, 6-2
with Amritraj–
Graham/Meister
(Australia/USA)
7-5, 6-4
with Amritraj–
Gerulaitis/McNamee
(USA/Australia)
6-7, 6-7

Grand Prix tournament, Milan
(25–31.3)
Becker–McEnroe (USA)
4-6, 3-6

Grand Prix tournament, Monte Carlo
(1–7.4)
Singles:
Becker–Nastase (Romania)
6-4, 6-1
Becker–Clerc (Argentina)
4-6, 3-6
Doubles:
with Lendl (Czechoslovakia)–
Clerc/Nastase
(Argentina/Romania)
6-7, 2-6

Invitation tournament, Houston
(15–21.4)
Becker–Boytin (USA)
6-1, 6-2
Becker–Wilander (Sweden)
3-6, 6-7

Grand Prix tournament, Atlanta
(22–28.4)
Singles:
Becker–Denton (USA)
7-6, 4-6, 6-7
Doubles:
with Pate (USA)–
Alexander/Warwick
(Australia)
6-3, 7-6
with Pate–
Cash/Fitzgerald (Australia)
4-6, 6-3, 6-7

Grand Prix tournament, Las Vegas
(29.4–5.5)
Singles:
Becker–Giammalva (USA)
7-5, 6-1

Becker–Edberg (Sweden)
6-3, 6-7, 6-2
Becker–Smid (Czechoslovakia)
4-6, 7-6, 6-7
Doubles:
with Pate (USA)–
Pfister/Testerman (USA)
7-6, 3-6, 6-4
with Pate–
Gilbert/van Patten (USA)
4-6, 6-2, 6-7

Italian Open, Rome
(13–19.5)
Singles:
Becker–Benhabiles (France)
6-3, 6-3
Becker–Tulasne (France)
6-3, 6-1
Becker–Aguilera (Spain)
7-6, 6-3
Becker–Gunnarson (Sweden)
4-6, 6-4, 6-3
Becker–Noah (France)
3-6, 3-6
Doubles:
with Noah (France)–
Dowdeswell/Soares
(England/Brazil)
6-3, 6-3
with Noah–
Ocleppo/Panatta (Italy)
6-2, 6-3

French Open, Paris
(27.5–9.6/Grand Slam)
Singles:
Becker–Gerulaitis (USA)
6-3, 6-7, 6-1, 6-1
Becker–Wilander (Sweden)
3-6, 2-6, 1-6

Grand Prix tournament, Queens
(10–16.6)
Singles:
Becker–Nelson (USA)
7-6, 7-5
Becker–Cassidy (USA)
6-4, 7-6
Becker–Pate (USA)
6-4, 6-7, 6-3
Becker–Cash (Australia)
6-4, 6-4
Becker–McNamee (Australia)
6-1, 6-4
Becker–Kriek (USA)
6-2, 6-3
Doubles:
with M. Leach (USA)–
Gonzalez/Mitchell
(Paraguay/USA)
5-7, 6-3, 3-6

**Wimbledon
(24.6–7.7/Grand Slam)**
Singles:
Becker–Pfister (USA)
4-6, 6-3, 6-2, 6-4
Becker–Anger (USA)
6-0, 6-1, 6-3
Becker–Nystrom (Sweden)
3-6, 7-6, 6-1, 4-6, 9-7
Becker–Mayotte (USA)
6-3, 4-6, 6-7, 7-6, 6-2
Becker–Leconte (France)
7-6, 3-6, 6-3, 6-4
Becker–Jarryd (Sweden)
2 6, 7-6, 6-3, 6-3
Becker–Curren (USA)
6-3, 6-7, 7-6, 6-4
Doubles:
With M. Leach (USA)–
Nystrom/Wilander (Sweden)
7-5, 6-3, 7-6
Dropped out 2nd round

**Grand Prix tournament,
Indianapolis
(22–28.7)**
Becker–Pernfors (Sweden)
4-6, 7-6, 6-2
Becker–Cancellotti (Italy)
6-4, 6-2
Becker–Mecir
(Czechoslovakia)
6-2, 7-5
Becker–Lendl
(Czechoslovakia)
7-5, 2-6, 2-6

**Davis Cup: 2nd round
v. USA 3-2
(2–4.8)**
Singles:
Becker–Teltscher
6-2, 6-2, 6-3
Becker–Krickstein
6-2, 6-2, 6-1
Doubles:
with Maurer–
Flach/Seguso
2-6, 8-6, 1-6, 6-4, 5-7

**Grand Prix tournament,
Kitzbühel
(5–11.8)**
Singles:
Becker–Perez (Uruguay)
3-6, 1-6
Doubles:
with Slozil (Czechoslovakia)–
Courteau/Tulasne (France)
6-4, 6-0
with Slozil–
Cane/Panatta (Italy)
4-6, 6-7

**Grand Prix tournament,
Cincinnati
(19–25.8)**
Becker–Perkis (Israel)
6-2, 6-3
Becker–Teacher (USA)
6-4, 6-4
Becker–Sadri (USA)
4-6, 6-1, 6-4
Becker–Pfister (USA)
5-7, 6-1, 6-4
Becker–Nystrom (Sweden)
6-4, 7-5
Becker–Wilander (Sweden)
6-4, 6-2

**US Open, Flushing Meadow,
New York
(27.8–8.9/Grand Slam)**
Singles:
Becker–Doohan (Australia)
6-4, 6-1, 6-2
Becker–van Boekel
(Netherlands)
6-3, 6-0, 6-2
Becker–Evernden
(New Zealand)
7-6, 6-3, 7-6
Becker–Nystrom (Sweden)
3-6, 4-6, 6-4, 4-6
Doubles:
with Zivojinovic (Yugoslavia)–
Di Laura/K. Jones (USA)
6-3, 6-2
with Zivojinovic–
Noah/Leconte (France)
7-6, 6-7, 6-7

**Exhibition match, Seattle
(10.9)**
Becker–Jensen (USA)
6-1, 6-3

**Exhibition match, Portland
(11.9)**
Becker–Noah (France)
7-6, 6-7, 6-2

**Exhibition match, Tulsa
(18/19.9)**
Becker–Gerulaitis (USA)
6-3, 6-3
Becker–Curren (USA)
6-7, 7-6, 6-3

**Exhibition match, Berlin
(21.9)**
Becker–Zivojinovic
(Yugoslavia)
6-3, 7-6

**Davis Cup: semi-finals
v. Czechoslovakia 5-0
(4–6.10)**
Singles:
Becker–Mecir
6-3, 7-5, 6-4
Becker–Pimek
6-1, 6-4
Doubles:
with Maurer–
Lendl/Smid
6-1, 7-5, 6-4

**Exhibition match,
Yokohama
(19.10)**
Becker–Vilas
7-6, 7-6, 6-3

**Exhibition match, Tokyo
(21.10)**
Becker–Connors (USA)
6-1, 6-2

**Grand Prix tournament,
Tokyo
(22–27.10)**
Singles:
Becker–Schultz (USA)
6-2, 6-0
Becker–Sadri (USA)
6-3, 6-1
Becker–Jarryd (Sweden)
7-6, 6-4
Becker–Lendl
(Czechoslovakia)
3-6, 6-7
Doubles:
with Zivojinovic (Yugoslavia)–
Kohlberg/Van't Hof (USA)
7-6 6-3
with Zivojinovic–
Gomez/Lendl
(Ecuador/Czechoslovakia)
6-7, 3-6

**Exhibition match,
Barcelona
(29.10)**
Becker–McEnroe (USA)
2-6, 5-7

**Invitation tournament,
Antwerp
(28.10–3.11)**
Becker–Gerulaitis (USA)
6-3, 6-4
Becker–Wilkison (USA)
6-2, 6-1
Becker–McEnroe (USA)
3-6, 4-6

**Exhibition match, Berlin
(4.11)**
Becker–Lendl
(Czechoslovakia)
6-2, 4-6, 4-6

**Exhibition match,
S'Hertogenbosch
(6.11)**
Becker–Lendl
(Czechoslovakia)
2-6, 6-3, 6-2

**Exhibition match,
Dusseldorf
(7.11)**
Becker–Lendl
(Czechoslovakia)
6-7, 6-4. 6-3

**Grand Prix tournament,
London
(12–17.11)**
Singles:
Becker–Glickstein (Israel)
6-2, 7-5
Becker–Bates (England)
7-5, 7-6
Becker–Leach (USA)
6-4, 5-3 (ret'd)
Becker–Jarryd (Sweden)
7-6, 7-6
Becker–Lendl
(Czechoslovakia)
7-6, 3-6, 6-4, 4-6, 4-6
Doubles:
with Zivojinovic (Yugoslavia)–
Gunnarson/Mortensen
(Sweden/Denmark)
6-0, 6-1
with Zivojinovic–
DePalmer/Donelly (USA)
3-6, 6-3, 6-2
with Zivojinovic–
Fleming/Van Rensburg
(USA/South Africa)
6-3, 6-4
with Zivojinovic–
Jarryd/Forget
(Sweden/France)
5-7, 6-4, 5-7

**Australian Open,
Melbourne
(25.11–8.12/Grand Slam)**
Singles:
Becker–Schapers
(Netherlands)
6-3, 4-6, 6-7, 6-4, 3-6
Doubles:
with Zivojinovic (Yugoslavia)–
Evernden/Testerman
(New Zealand/USA)
7-6, 2-2 (ret'd)
with Zivojinovic–
Bates/Mansdorf
(England/Israel)
6-4, 6-4
with Zivojinovic–
Annacone/van Rensburg
(USA/South Africa)
7-5, 6-7, 7-5, 6-7, 7-9

**Davis Cup: final
v. Sweden 2-3
(20–22.12)**
Singles:
Becker–Edberg
6-3, 3-6, 7-5, 8-6
Becker–Wilander
6-3, 2-6, 6-3, 6-3
Doubles:
with Maurer–
Wilander/Nystrom
4-6, 2-6, 1-6

ALL MATCHES 1986

Young Masters (indoors), Berlin
(1–5.1)
Becker–J. Brown (USA)
6-7, 6-2, 6-4
Becker–P. Lundgren (Sweden)
6-4, 7-5
Becker–Vajda
(Czechoslovakia)
6-3, 6-2
Becker–Sanchez (Spain)
6-4, 6-4
Becker–Wilander (Sweden)
6-1, 7-6, 6-0

Masters tournament (indoors), New York
(15–19.1)
Becker–Annacone (USA)
3-6, 6-3, 6-2
Becker–Wilander (Sweden)
6-4, 4-6, 6-3
Becker–Jarryd (Sweden)
6-3, 6-4
Becker–Lendl
(Czechoslovakia)
2-6, 6-7, 3-6

Grand Prix tournament, Boca West
(10–23.2)
Singles:
Becker–Nijssen (Netherlands)
6-3, 7-5
Becker–Slozil (Czechoslovakia)
6-4, 6-4
Becker–Srejber
(Czechoslovakia)
6-7, 3-6
Doubles:
with Zivojinovic (Yugoslavia)–
Pernfors/Sadri (Sweden/USA)
6-3, 5-7, 6-1
with Zivojinovic–
Cassidy/Purcell (USA)
6-3, 6-1
with Zivojinovic–
Meister/Wittus (USA)
6-4, 6-7, 7-6
with Zivojinovic–
S. Davis/Pate (USA)
7-6, 6-2
with Zivojinovic–
Edberg/Jarryd (Sweden)
7-6, 4-6, 6-7, 3-6

Grand Prix tournament, La Quinta
(24.2–2.3)
Becker–M. Leach (USA)
6-3, 6-3
Becker–Higueras (Spain)
6-2, 6-4

Becker–Nystrom (Sweden)
6-7, 2-6
Doubles:
with Zivojinovic (Yugoslavia)–
Popp/Perkis (West
Germany/Israel)
6-4, 7-6
with Zivojinovic–
R. Leach/Pawsat (USA)
6-7, 7-6, 6-0
with Zivojinovic–
Graham/Testerman
(Australia/USA)
4-6, 6-4, 6-3
with Zivojinovic–
Noah/Stewart (France/USA)
2-6, 1-6

Davis Cup: 1st round v. Mexico 2-3
(7–9.3)
Singles:
Becker–Lavalle
6-3, 6-2, 6-4
Becker–Maciel
6-3, 6-1, 6-1
Doubles:
with Maurer–
Lavalle/Perez-Pascal
6-3, 1-6, 5-7, 6-3, 4-6

Exhibition match (indoors), Innsbruck
(15.3)
Becker–Noah (France)
4-6, 6-3, 3-6

Exhibition match (indoors), Stuttgart
(16.3)
Becker–Noah (France)
6-4, 6-2

Grand Prix tournament (indoors), Brussels
(17–23.3)
Singles:
Becker–Dyke (Australia)
3-6, 3-6
Doubles:
with Zivojinovic (Yugoslavia)–
Edmondson/Warwick
(Australia)
6-2, 6-7, 6-2
with Zivojinovic–
Evernden/Leconte
(New Zealand/France)
6-4, 6-3
with Zivojinovic–
Casal/Sanchez (Spain)
6-4, 6-4

with Zivojinovic–
Fitzgerald/Smid
(Australia/Czechoslovakia)
7-6, 7-5

Grand Prix tournament (indoors), Chicago
(24–30.3)
Singles:
Becker–M. Leach (USA)
6-3, 6-1
Becker–Sadri (USA)
6-4, 7-6
Becker–Annacone (USA)
6-4, 6-4
Becker–Connors (USA)
7-6, 4-6, 6-4
Becker–Lendl
(Czechoslovakia)
7-6, 6-3
Doubles:
with M. Leach (USA)–
Gilbert/van Patten (USA)
6-3, 6-1
with M. Leach–
Michibata/Pearce
(Canada/USA)
6-2, 3-6, 6-7

Grand Prix tournament (indoors), Atlanta
(31.3–6.4)
Singles:
Becker–Wilkison (USA)
2-6, 6-2, 1-6
Doubles:
with Cash (Australia)–
Meister/Teltscher (USA)
7-6, 6-4
with Cash–
Kohlberg/van't Hof (USA)
6-3, 6-7, 4-6

Exhibition match (indoors), Washington
(8.4)
Becker–Vilas (Argentina)
6-4, 7-5

WCT World Championships (indoors), Dallas
(7–13.4)
Becker–Annacone (USA)
7-5, 7-5, 6-1
Becker–Edberg (Sweden)
7-6, 7-6, 4-6, 7-6
Becker–Jarryd (Sweden)
7-6, 1-6, 1-6, 4-6

Exhibition match (indoors), Kiel
(28.4)
Becker–Noah (France)
6-3, 6-7, 6-3

Exhibition match (indoors), Kaarst
(29–31.4)
Becker–Leconte (France)
4-6, 7-6, 6-7

Exhibition match, Nimes
(1.5)
Becker–Leconte (France)
6-4, 6-2
Becker–Wilander (Sweden)
4-6, 3-6

Grand Prix tournament, Forest Hills
(5–11.5)
Singles:
Becker–Aguilera (Spain)
6-2, 6-4
Becker–Edwards
(South Africa)
6-4, 6-1
Becker–de la Pena (Argentina)
7-5, 7-5
Becker–Jaite (Argentina)
2-6, 6-7
Doubles:
with Zivojinovic (Yugoslavia)–
Cox/Fancutt (USA/Australia)
7-5, 6-3
with Zivojinovic–
Giammalva/Willenborg (USA)
6-3, 7-5
with Zivojinovic–
Gilbert/Teacher (USA)
6-2, 6-2
with Zivojinovic–
Gunnarson/Nystrom (Sweden)
7-5, 6-7, 6-4
with Zivojinovic–
Gildemeister/Gomez
(Chile/Ecuador)
6-7, 6-7

Italian Open, Rome
(12–18.5)
Singles:
Becker–Westphal
(West Germany)
6-2, 6-0
Becker–de la Pena(Argentina)
6-2, 6-3
Becker–Lavalle (Mexico)
6-1, 6-3
Becker–Sanchez (Spain)
3-6, 4-6

Doubles:
with Zivojinovic (Yugoslavia)–
Nastase/Panatta
(Romania/Italy)
6-1, 6-2
with Zivojinovic–
J. Svensson/Pimek
(Sweden/Czechoslovakia)
6-4, 6-0
with Zivojinovic–
Gildemeister/Gomez
(Chile/Ecuador)
4-6, 4-6

French Open, Paris
(26.5–8.6/Grand Slam)
Becker–Potier (France)
6-0, 6-3, 6-0
Becker–Oresar (Yugoslavia)
6-2, 6-0, 6-7, 6-3
Becker–Teltscher (USA)
6-3, 6-3, 5-7, 6-4
Becker–Sanchez (Spain)
6-0, 4-6, 4-6, 6-4, 6-2
Becker–Pernfors (Sweden)
6-2, 4-6, 2-6, 0-6

Grand Prix tournament,
Queens
(9–15.6)
Singles:
Becker–Flach (USA)
6-2, 6-2
Becker–Chesnokov (USSR)
6-4, 6-2
Becker–Youl (Australia)
6-3, 6-1
Becker–Mayotte (USA)
7-6, 6-7, 2-6
Doubles:
with Zivojinovic (Yugoslavia)–
Gilbert/Teacher (USA)
6-4, 7-6
Dropped out 2nd round

Wimbledon
(23.6–6.7/Grand Slam)
Becker–Benqoechea
(Argentina)
6-4, 6-2, 6-1
Becker–Tom Gullikson (USA)
6-4, 6-3, 6-2
Becker–McNamee (Australia)
6-4, 6-4, 4-6, 6-4
Becker–Pernfors (Sweden)
6-4, 7-6, 6-2
Becker–Mecir
(Czechoslovakia)
6-4, 6-2, 7-6
Becker–Leconte (France)
6-2, 6-4, 6-7, 6-3
Becker–Lendl
(Czechoslovakia)
6-4, 6-3, 7-5

Exhibition tournament,
Majorca
(14/15.7)
Becker–Sundstrom (Sweden)
3-6, 6-7
Becker–Tulasne (France)
6-2. 6-4

Grand Prix tournament,
Stratton Mountain
(4–10.8)
Singles:
Becker–Schultz (USA)
6-4, 7-6
Becker–Flach (USA)
6-4, 6-7, 6-4
Becker–Curren (USA)
6-2, 3-6, 7-6
Becker–Laurendeau (Canada)
7-5, 6-2
Becker–McEnroe (USA)
3-6, 7-5, 7-5
Becker–Lendl
(Czechoslovakia)
4-6, 6-7
Doubles:
with Wilkison (USA)–
Kratzman/Mansdorf
(Australia/Israel)
7-6, 6-4
with Wilkison–
Connors/Goldie (USA)
6-3, 6-3
with Wilkison–
van Patten/Gilbert (USA)
7-5, 4-6, 3-6

Grand Prix tournament,
Toronto
(11–17.8)
Singles:
Becker–Krickstein (USA)
6-2, 6-1
Becker–Maciel (Mexico)
6-3, 6-3
Becker–Schultz (USA)
6-4, 7-6
Becker–Canter (USA)
7-6, 7-6
Becker–Edberg (Sweden)
6-4, 3-6, 6-3
Doubles:
with Zivojinovic (Yugoslavia)–
Doohan/Wilkison (USA)
6-4, 6-2
with Zivojinovic–
Acuna/Green (Chile/USA)
6-3, 6-4
with Zivojinovic–
Forget/Noah (France)
6-4, 5-7, 6-2
with Zivojinovic–
Hooper/Leach (USA)
7-6, 3-6, 3-6

US Open, Flushing Meadow,
New York
(25.8–7.9/Grand Slam)
Becker–Michibata (Canada)
6-2, 6-7, 6-4, 6-2
Becker–Motta (Brazil)
6-3, 6-0, 6-2
Becker–Casal (Spain)
7-5, 6-4, 6-2
Becker–Donnelly (USA)
6-4, 6-3, 6-7, 6-4
Becker–Srejber
(Czechoslovakia)
6-3, 6-2, 6-1
Becker–Mecir
(Czechoslovakia)
6-4, 3-6, 4-6, 6-3, 3-6

German Open, Hamburg
(15–21.9)
Singles:
Becker–Purcell (USA)
5-7, 6-2, 6-7
Doubles:
with Jelen (West Germany)–
Segarceanu/Westphal
(Romania/West Germany)
6-4, 6-3
with Jelen–
Gunnarsson/Nystrom
(Sweden)
7-5, 6-1
with Jelen–
Motta/Willenborg
(Brazil/USA)
4-6, 7-5, 6-3
with Jelen–
Bathman/Schapers
(Sweden/Netherlands)
6-2, 6-4
with Jelen–
Casal/Sanchez (Spain)
4-6, 1-6

Davis Cup: relegation
play-off
v. Ecuador 5-0
Essen (3–5.10)
Singles:
Becker–Viver
6-4, 6-4, 10-8
Becker–Gomez
7-5, 6-2
Doubles:
with Jelen–
Gomez/Viver
6-2, 6-4, 6-4

Grand Prix tournament,
Sydney
(13–19.10)
Singles:
Becker–Maasdorp (South
Africa)
6-1, 6-3
Becker–Fitzgerald (Australia)
6-4, 7-5

Becker–Dyke (Australia)
6-4, 6-4
Becker–Layendecker (USA)
6-4, 6-4
Becker–Lendl
(Czechoslovakia)
3-6, 7-6, 6-2, 6-0
Doubles:
with Fitzgerald (Australia)–
Freeman/Nelson (USA)
6-4, 6-1
with Fitzgerald–
Cash/Woodforde (Australia)
6-3, 6-3
with Fitzgerald–
Drewett/Warwick (Australia)
6-4, 7-6
with Fitzgerald–
McNamara/McNamee
(Australia)
6-4, 7-6

Grand Prix tournament,
Tokyo
(20–26.10)
Singles:
Becker–Anger (USA)
6-3, 6-4
Becker–Yzaga (Ecuador)
6-3, 6-2
Becker–Annacone (USA)
6-2, 6-4
Becker–Connors (USA)
7-6, 2-6, 6-3
Becker–Edberg (Sweden)
7-6, 6-1
Doubles:
with Jelen (West Germany)–
Bates/Derlin
(England/New Zealand)
7-6, 6-1
Gomez/Lendl
(Ecuador/Czechoslovakia)
4-6, 5-7

Grand Prix tournament,
Paris
(27.10–2.11)
Singles:
Becker–Nunez (Argentina)
7-5, 6-4
Becker–Curren (USA)
6-2, 6-4
Becker–J. Svensson (Sweden)
6-4, 6-4
Becker–Leconte (France)
6-2, 3-6, 6-3
Becker–Casal (Spain)
6-4, 6-3, 7-6
Doubles:
with Zivojinovic (Yugoslavia)–
Steyn/Visser (South Africa)
7-6, 4-6, 4-6

**Exhibition tournament, Atlanta
(24–30.11)**
Round Robin:
Becker–McEnroe (USA)
6-3, 5-7, 7-5
Becker–Wilander (Sweden)
7-6, 6-3
Becker–Gilbert (USA)
6-7, 6-4, 3-6
Play-offs:
Becker–Noah (France)
6-4, 6-3
Becker–McEnroe
3-6, 6-3, 7-5

**Masters tournament
(indoors), New York
(1–7.12)**
Round Robin:
Becker–Nystrom (Sweden)
6-1, 6-3
Becker–Leconte (France)
0-6, 6-1, 6-1
Becker–Wilander (Sweden)
6-3, 3-6, 6-3
Play-offs:
Becker–Edberg (Sweden)
6-4, 6-4
Becker–Lendl
(Czechoslovakia)
4-6, 4-6, 4-6

**Young Masters (indoors),
Stuttgart
(10–14.12)**
Round Robin:
Becker–Vysand (USSR)
6-3, 6-2
Becker–Canter (USA)
6-4, 6-1
Becker–Chesnokov (USSR)
2-6, 6-4, 6-7
Play-offs:
Becker–Jelen (West Germany)
6-3, 6-4
Becker–J. Svensson (Sweden)
7-6, 7-6, 6-3